Surf and Saltwater Fishing in the Carolinas

Jeffrey Weeks

Surf and Saltwater Fishing in the Carolinas

Copyright © 2011 by Jeffrey Weeks

www.surfandsalt.com

ISBN 1463778228

This book is dedicated to my dad, Dr. Donnie E. Weeks, who first took me saltwater fishing all those long years ago.

Acknowledgments

I'd like to thank just a few of the many who have fished with me or helped me learn about fishing and life over the years, in person, through books, and on the internet: Jimmy Simpson, Captain Patrick Kelly (Captain Smiley), Captain Mark Dickson, Captain Rick Caton, Captain Steven Prevatte, CH Laughridge and all the posters on NC Waterman (especially Scott Hobbs, Ray Brown, ncpierman, Baitwaister, seastreet, bakesta, redfish, Fishing Fool, downeaster, dontcatchmany, seawolftoo, Mechanic Bob, sea byrd and many others), Chris Elkins, Bobby White, CCA-NC, Al Raynor, Richard Phelps, the folks at the Ocean Crest Pier, the folks at the Bogue Inlet Pier, the folks at the Ocean Isle Fishing Center, my grandmother Lula Jane Weeks, my uncle Tony Weeks for the 'shark' story, Neil and Chuck Taft for helping me learn so much, the folks at the *Brunswick Beacon* newspaper (especially Stacey Manning and Michael Paul), Renee Sloan, the folks at Pier and Surf.com, the kids from North Moore High School in Robbins who helped me compose my first little Surf and Salt book over a decade ago, Elaine Wright for letting me fish out of her house so many times, John Teeters and Lane Benton for the 'trailer bait' story, Dr. Scott Huffmon (remember that long ago unbelievable spot run on the Ocean Isle Pier?), my mother Michelle Denton and Ed, dad and Terri, two amazing children named Josh and Jordie, my soul mate Jennifer Wahab, and my wonderful daughters Elanor and Zelda.

Special thanks to my sister Windy Remer who has listened to me talk about nothing but fishing and baseball her entire life.

I also salute those wonderful Carolina fishing writers whose books and articles inspired me to write this book…Mike Marsh, Bob Goldstein, Bob Newman, Jerry Dilsaver, Craig Holt, Ty Conti, Dan Kibler, Donald Millus, Joe Malat, the legendary Joel Arrington, and of course Dr. Bogus.

A big thanks to all the US military servicemen and women whose sacrifice over the years has made our freedom to fish possible. For information and links to organizations like MAD and FISH that help take veterans fishing in the Carolinas see the Cyberfishing chapter at the end of this book or email me at saltyweeks@gmail.com.

Foreword by Captain Smiley

Growing up as an angler along the North Myrtle Beach Grand Strand I took the great fishing for granted, thinking that it was this good everywhere. As I have become more experienced and fished many exotic places I have come to realize that the Carolinas have some of the best fishing in the world.

Our bountiful waters are full of life including fish, shellfish, birds, reptiles, and mammals…all of which lie in a pristine environment. Fishing here is an exceptional experience that I love to share with clients in search of the perfect catch.

Guiding for a living in the Carolinas is the best job a person can have. Every day is a new adventure. Just seeing the sunrise and sunset over the ocean and the beaches is a religion in itself. The excitement of hearing your reel screaming as a redfish pulls across a mudflat will install a memory in your mind you will never forget.

But the most fascinating and important part of fishing in the Carolinas is the people. It seems as if you really are in a Jimmy Buffett song. Friendly waves as fellow boaters pass. The local commercial fishermen working crab pots and nets. Stories the old timers tell about the ways things used to be.

The people that fish these waters are generally happy people. It is truly a special paradise full of smiling faces and beautiful places.

Captain Patrick Kelly
North Myrtle Beach, SC

Photo Credits

Front cover photo:

The picture on the front features Captain Patrick Kelly of Captain Smiley Fishing Charters and Hannah Maupin with a nice speckled trout caught in the North Myrtle Beach region.

Other photos:

Many of the photos in this book were provided by Captain Patrick Kelly of Captain Smiley Fishing Charters. You can find him on the internet at http://www.captainsmileyfishingcharters.com or call him at 843-361-7445.

Other photos were provided by Captain Mark Dickson of Shallow Minded Inshore Guide Service. You can find him on the internet at http://www.fishmyrtlebeach.com or call him at 843-458-3055.

Some pictures were taken by the staff of the Ocean Crest Fishing Pier at Oak Island, NC.
You can find this great fishing pier on the internet at http://www.oceancrestpiernc.com or call them at 910-278-6674.

All of the other photos were taken by me or sent to me by folks who gave me the rights to publication.

Table of Contents

1. Carolina Saltwater Fishing.. 1

2. How to Catch Flounder... 7

3. How to Catch Redfish.. 11

4. How to Catch Speckled Trout.. 15

5. How to Catch Bluefish... 19

6. How to Catch Spanish Mackerel.. 23

7. How to Catch Pompano 25

8. How to Catch Spot 29

9. How to Catch Croaker 33

10. How to Catch Black Drum... 35

11. How to Catch Sea Mullet... 39

12. How to Catch Sheepshead 43

13. A Carolina Angler's Guide to Inshore Scented Soft Baits 47

14. A Guide to Carolina Fishing Rigs....................................... 51

15. Using MirrOlures to Catch Speckled Trout and Redfish............. 55

16. Tips for Targeting Big Doormat Flounder............................. 59

17. Winter Saltwater Fishing in the Carolinas 63

18. Dark Secrets: Night Fishing in the Carolinas 67

19. Tips for Catching Live Bait 71

20. Using Tandem Rigs for Spring Trout and Summer Shad............. 75

21. Saltwater Tactics: Trolling for Flounder Against the Tide.......... 79

22. Saltwater Tips: Catching Spring Redfish.............................. 83

23. Saltwater Tips: Using Live Shrimp to Catch Speckled Trout....... 87

24. Surf Fishing Tips: What to Use for Bait 91

25. Carolina Pier Fishing 95

26. The Best Carolina Seafood Recipes............................ 99

27. Carolina Kayak Fishing 143

28. Summertime Carolina Shark Fishing............................ 145

29. Backwater and Inlet Shore Fishing Tips 147

30. Catching Fall Spot on Fishbites Artificial Bloodworms............ 151

31. Two Funny Carolina Fishing Stories 153

32. Saltwater Secrets: Catching Spanish on a Gold Hook Rig 159

33. Saltwater Secrets: Push Poling for Winter Redfish 163

34. Tips for Taking a Kid Fishing.................................. 167

35. Cyberfishing: Where to Get Current Fishing Reports and Tips . 171

1. Carolina Saltwater Fishing

Great coastal angling opportunities abound in North and South Carolina for both the locals who know the waters well and the tourists who want to get in a little fishing while on their vacation at the beach. Whether you wish to fish from a pier, the shore, or a small boat, our inshore saltwater scene provides terrific action that is more interactive and more rewarding for young and old than sitting at home watching television or playing video games. It is also the perfect way for an aspiring fisherman to spend the day while the rest of their family soaks up the atmosphere at the crowded nearby beaches.

Carolina waters are home to many fish that are highly sought after for their fighting ability on the line and their great taste on the dinner table. One of the most sought after fish in these parts is the flounder. Two different species of flounder dwell in our waters, the summer and the southern, with the summer flounder (called fluke up north) being most common on the ocean side and the southern flounder caught most often inshore. The majority of fishermen cannot tell the difference between the two; they are just happy to catch a tasty flounder.

Flounder lie on the bottom, with a totally white side resting in the sand. They have both eyes on the other side, the brown side, of their heads and sit with them pointed upwards watching for live minnows and shrimp to come within reach. Then they strike with surprising speed, rising up from the bottom to grasp their prey with a mouth full of small teeth.

Most people fish for flounder with live bait. On piers fishermen toss mud minnows around the pilings in shallow waters. Shore and surf anglers often cast and slowly retrieve finger mullet to entice them. Flounder fishermen in boats drift with the tide or troll, crossing vast stretches of sand and pulling minnows on the bottom.

You can also anchor up near structure and cast live bait or artificial lures like jigs and grubs to them. Flounder will hit still-fished bait such as cut mullet or shrimp on occasion. At night, gigging flounder with spears is a traditional and popular Carolina pastime. Flounder are not spectacular fighters but are regarded as one of the best tasting fish to come from our waters.

Another very popular fish is the speckled trout. Specks hit throughout the year, with early spring and fall probably being the best times to fish for them. There are always some around, however. Specks can be caught many ways, but as with flounder a live or moving bait is what works in most cases.

The best bait for speckled trout is live shrimp, fished either under a float or on a rig without much weight. Local bait shops only have shrimp available at certain times of the year, though, and they are not cheap. Many fishermen use cast nets to catch their own in the creeks. Shrimp are not present in the colder months. Even if you have them, there are times when the small, bait-stealing pinfish will eat your shrimp before the trout see it.

Specks can also be caught on a variety of lures, fished slowly in cold water and faster as the temperature rises. The Gulp brand has many gained many followers in recent years, as have the DOA and Billy Bay Halo shrimp-imitation lures, and there are literally hundreds of different kinds of grubs and jigs that will work for trout if they are in a feeding mood. Trout put up a good fight and have delicate white meat that is very good fried but also great in many other fish recipes.

Another important Carolina inshore fish is the feisty panfish called the spot. Spot are the most anticipated fish of the year, present in some numbers all the time but swarming onto the beaches in great schools during the fall. Piers fill up at this time for the annual spot run as anglers participate in what is truly a long-time tradition handed down through generations. In addition to the piers, spot are caught from small boats in the inlets, from the surf, and from the shore around bridges and in the waterways.

Although spot are not large, they are a great tasting little fish. Everybody fries spot, and none are ever wasted. Although the runs are unpredictable, when spot are active they can be caught on bottom rigs two at a time. Fall spot often sport bright yellow fins due to their active hormones during this time, leading to the term 'yellow-bellied' spot. Big 'yellow-bellied' spot fight surprising well for a panfish.

Spot are caught mainly on bloodworms, earthworms, and cut shrimp. Bloodworms are expensive, and in recent years, the synthetic bloodworm strips offered by the company Fishbites have gained popularity, because spot hit them as well as the real thing, but these new tougher baits stay on the hook longer. Earthworms, however, are still a very popular and cheap alternative.

Redfish (known in many places as red drum, and by a lot of other local names) are common in our waters, with smaller drum called puppy drum present almost everywhere. Out on the famed Outer Banks anglers aim for big red drum in the 40 to 60 pounds range. These fish are known as channel bass to old timers. The catches of these big drum are one reason that red drum are NC's official state saltwater fish. Redfish hit all kinds of natural baits, and puppy drum strike the same lures as trout.

The bulky black drum, close cousins to the redfish, are not as appreciated as their relatives but are very good eating if they aren't too big. Black drum feed on the bottom near any bridge or other structure with barnacles and will hit baits of shrimp or other shellfish.

In the surf and on the piers bluefish, slashing brutes with angry attitudes, hit cut bait or thin pencil plugs such as the Gotcha brand, often with the color red on them. Out a little farther, beautiful and sleek Spanish mackerel strike rapidly retrieved silver and gold lures zipped through the blue water.

Pier and surf fishermen can also catch other tasty panfish like pompano, sea mullet (whiting), and croaker. Many of the fish caught in the waterway or on the pier are great for eating. In the case of trophy fish, like the larger red drum, anglers will release the fish when the fight is over.

Remember that many of the important game and food fish such as flounder, specks, and red drum are protected by strict size and creel limits. Also if you are fishing from the surf, shore, or a boat you must have a fishing license in both states. Most piers have a blanket license to cover you, as do most fishing guides.

If you are a visitor to the area and don't have fishing gear, the two easiest options are to head to a local pier, where you can rent everything you need and fish on the spot, or contact a fishing guide and set up a trip. Although piers seem to be disappearing from the Carolina coast at an alarming rate, we still have some good ones along the coast, as well as lots of great fishing guides who can hook you up while providing everything you need for an enjoyable day on the water.

The internet is a great place for more information about all these fish species, for finding tips about how to catch them, and for discovering the different inshore fishing tactics and trends folks are discussing right now. You can find plenty of information and links on my own blog and website: **A Dash of Salty** and **Surf and Salt**. The urls are below.

Don't sit in front of the computer too long, however; get out and do some interactive research of your own. If you come to the beaches for a vacation, don't forget about the great fishing going on around you.

www.saltyweeks.blogspot.com
www.surfandsalt.com

2. How to Catch Flounder

Flounder are a premier food fish sought by recreational and commercial fishermen in the Carolinas. The coast of North and South Carolina is home to two main species of flounder: the southern flounder that inhabits mainly inlets and backwaters, and the summer flounder that prefers the ocean waters. Both species overlap and are caught by identical methods.

Flounder are flatfish with both eyes on the darker side of their head. They lie quietly on the ocean floor with their white side down, practically camouflaged in anticipation of ambushing any baitfish, shrimp, crab, or other small creature that scurries above or below them. Flounder congregate near structure, like pilings and oyster bars, or over vast stretches of mud and sand bottoms. They like a strong tide where the current will bring food in range.

Flounder favor water temperature over 60 degrees and are most numerous in the Carolinas between April and November. They winter offshore, which is also where they breed.

Bottom fishing with a rounded weigh, wide-gap (Kahle) or circle hook, and live bait is the premier flounder technique. They spread out around moving water and structure, so the best method is to keep the bait moving or within inches of the bottom.

A fishfinder rig with an egg or bullet sinker is hard to beat for flounder. Use 8 to 10 lb test line on a 6 6" to 8 foot rod. On the line side run a ½ to 2 ounce egg weight (depending on the strength of current) and tie on a swivel to stop the sinker. Add 15 to 22 inches of 20 or 25 lb monofilament as leader. Some flounder experts like fluorocarbon leaders instead. Tie on a number 1 to 5/0 Kahle or circle hook (based on the size of the flounder biting) and go get them.

Live minnows such as finger mullet, peanut pogies, or mud minnows are the top flounder takers. Hook the minnow through the lips or just above the eye sockets. Live shrimp is also a reliable bait but pesky bait-stealers like pinfish and crabs may make shrimp a poor choice. Shrimp should be hooked in the head, but avoid the dark brain area.

With live bait you have to give the flounder time to take the bait. Flounder hit a minnow to stun it and then take it in their mouth and roll it around a bit. They even will scale it with their small sharp teeth. If you strike too soon you will get back a scaled minnow. Some anglers wait as much as two minutes. I usually try to count to 30 slowly, then hit the fish. If the minnow comes back to you with just the belly eaten out you have been the victim of a blue crab mauling and not a flounder strike.

Strips of fresh cut bait from squid or any fresh fish will work, although today more anglers use the artificial bait strips (many of them synthetic and flavored) available for flounder fishing in the tackle shops. Fishbites is a good brand and there are others. Strip bait and artificial bait strips must be in motion, either used when drifting or dragged with a slow retrieve.

Flounder will occasionally hit cut shrimp, squid, or bloodworms still-fished by bottom fishermen. The biggest flounder I have caught to this point was a 31 inch monster flatfish that hit an earthworm while I was spot fishing around midnight at the old Sunset Beach Bridge. No lie. I was on the rocks and had no landing net, so I had to jump in the waterway and swim that sucker to shore.

Summer and southern flounder average a few pounds each, although 'doormat' flounder of over 5 pounds are often caught by anglers. The North Carolina state record flounder is 20 lbs, 8 ounces caught in 1980 at Carolina Beach and the South Carolina state record flounder is 17 lbs, 6 ounces caught in South Santee in 1974. Both fish were southern flounder, which get larger than summer flounder.

Pay attention to size and creel limits on flounder. Size limits get higher every year and creel limits get smaller. Some folks believe this is wise fisheries management, but I have always wondered if by doing this we are targeting the big females too much. In any case, check the regulations and don't break the rules.

3. How to Catch Redfish

Redfish are better known to many Carolina residents as red drum, and they have the singular distinction of being the official state saltwater fish of North Carolina. They have acquired tons of regional names over the years. Some folks call them spottail bass and the smaller ones are often referred to as puppy drum. Big Outer Banks fish have long been known in NC as channel bass. Whatever you call them, they are a beautiful and hard-fighting saltwater species.

Redfish are year-round residents in most parts of the Carolinas, schooling up in the winter in huge inshore pods and sticking it out as roaming marauders of mullet and menhaden even in the hottest summers. North Carolina has a famed population of huge bull red drum fish that visit the surf of the Outer Banks and have made places like Cape Hatteras, Ocracoke, and Nags Head world famous fishing spots. The rest of the Carolinas have plenty of smaller redfish in the creeks, waterways, inlets, and surf.

Tackle differs for big drum and smaller redfish. For the average redfish you need fishfinder or drum bottom rigs with two or three ounces of weight. Inshore anglers use egg sinkers while surf fishermen like pyramid and bank sinkers. Rods of 7 to 9 feet spooled with 8 to 12 lb test line are fine. Set your drag loose as red drum hammer baits when they hit.

For big Outer Banks channel bass you need specialized equipment. Custom-made rods 10 to 13 feet are common and 20 to 30 lb line is spooled on the reels. Many drum anglers use the new braids and fluorocarbon lines. Drum rigs typically have short heavy mono leaders leading to large hooks from 3/0 to 7/0 and utilize big weights from 4 to 8 ounces. Casting these rigs is an art in itself. In some places there are regulations on how long big drum rigs must be, and the use of circle hooks is required. Outer Banks tackle stores are the places to go to get rigged up, and there are some good internet links to follow in the Cyberfishing chapter of this book.

The best baits for redfish are small live finger mullet and fresh cut mullet. But redfish are accommodating and hit lots of baits such as live mud minnows, peanut pogies, pinfish, and spot as well as any kind of cut fish, fresh cut shrimp, squid, fiddler crabs, sand fleas, halved blue crabs, clam meat, bloodworms and even earthworms. Redfish will sometimes jerk the rod out of an unsuspecting spot angler's hands as they fish cut shrimp or bloodworms on the bottom. That's why you keep a light drag.

Large Outer Banks channel bass like big bloody cut baits such as cut mullet, spot heads, or strips of fresh menhaden or bluefish. The most important consideration is that your cut bait is fresh so it attracts big drum.

Many redfish are taken on lures. They love the scented soft baits like Gulp lures fished slowly and hopped off the bottom. Red drum also strike shrimp-imitating lures with gusto and respond to today's popular saltwater scent sprays.

They have long been caught on bucktail jigs. Lots of redfish pros take them on slowly-worked gold and silver spoons, MirrOlures, crankbaits, spinnerbaits, and a wide variety of plugs.

Redfish are good eating and yield thick white meat fillets, but they are highly regulated. The blackened redfish crazy of the 1980s nearly killed them off in the Gulf and the Atlantic, so they are closely watched by both the states and the federal government. Make sure you know the size and creel limits if you are going to keep a redfish. The world record red drum was a 94 lb, 2 oz fish taken in 1984 at Avon village on Cape Hatteras, NC.

4. How to Catch Speckled Trout

Speckled trout are among the most beautiful and sought after inshore fish of the Carolinas. Specks are an aggressive schooling fish, unpredictable but often occurring in big numbers. They will hit a wide variety of baits and lures but generally prefer live bait and moving offerings. Trout are also well known to be hard to please at times, like high-maintenance women (or men, I suppose).

Speckled trout are available in Carolina waters year-round, but sometimes only for those who know how to find them. They spawn in the spring, using the ocean surf and the inlet waterways as passages for their spawning runs. Trout roam in search of food, but schools will often station themselves near hard structure or inlet mouths as feeding zones.

Speckled trout feed heavily on shrimp and small fish. Studies show that shrimp makes up the largest percentage of the diet of most speckled trout, but that the larger trout (all females) prefer live fish like mullet and pogies. These large specks tend to be loners and will even gobble up little trout.

Specks are most active in water over 56 degrees, but can sometimes be caught in water as low as 48 degrees. In winter they school inshore or just off the beach. During this time they favor deep holes, especially around places near shallow water where bait gathers. Specks are intolerant of extreme cold and very harsh winters can cause trout stuns or kills in the Carolinas. For this reason the state regulatory agencies watch them closely. NC has even closed the season on trout harvest totally after a particularly bad winter kill.

Specks can be caught in many ways. Live bait fished under a float (usually live shrimp) is the top method, although live bait can also be fished on the bottom for them. The sliding depth of float rigs allows you to experiment and find out where they are feeding. Float rigs can be bought in coastal tackle shops or made with simple materials. There is a section on float rigs for trout later in this book.

Specks have only a few prominent front teeth and wire spooks them, so use fluorocarbon or heavy mono line as leader material and shun wire. Fishing line of 6 to 8 lbs is sufficient, and rods should be 6 6" to 9 feet in length. Try to avoid a lot of weight; just use a few split shot if you can. You may have to go up to a 2 or 3 ounce egg weight if necessary.

Specks love live shrimp. However, so do a lot of things and live shrimp is not always practical or available. The next best alternative is live finger mullet, or other minnows like peanut pogies (small menhaden), pinfish, or mud minnows. Many anglers don't know it, but big trout love to hit small pinfish. Big female trout will also gobble up small spot, croaker, and bluefish.

Cut bait drifted or dragged as in flounder fishing will work. Specks sometimes hit cut bait such as shrimp, squid, bloodworms, or cut fish on the bottom, but they don't do this as much as gray trout (weakfish) do and this is not the best way to target them.

Speckled trout are celebrated artificial lure takers. Many anglers these days use the Gulp line of synthetic baits or shrimp-imitations like the DOA or Billy Bay Halo Shrimp. There are many grub styles available for trout and all of them work on occasion. Green, chartreuse, white, and pink are top color choices. Trout can be tempted by double jig rigs that use a smaller jig as the trailing lure.

Hard lures such as the famous MirrOlure plugs are also effective and target larger trout. Bucktails and silver spoons will work. Surf anglers favor these weightier lures for casting distance. There are later chapters in the book dealing with speckled trout and lure selection.

Many different retrieves are used to target trout when fishing lures, and sometimes you must change and experiment. The big rule: the colder the water the slower you retrieve. In the dead of winter sometimes you don't need to retrieve at all (this is called deadsticking). Usually if trout are there and you are not catching them, you are retrieving too fast.

Specks average a few pounds each. The NC state record is 12 lbs, 4 ounces caught in Wrightsville Beach in 1961. The big ones are all females.

5. How to Catch Bluefish

Bluefish are the marauders of the Carolina coast, spreading fear and paranoia in smaller-sized fish wherever they go. Bluefish are common along the ocean beaches where large schools of blues, all similar in length to avoid cannibalistic comrades, feed attacking any bait in sight.

Bluefish also roam the inlets and marsh areas, although with less frequency. They can often be detected by watching feeding birds, which hover over bluefish schools picking up the remains of unfortunate baitfish.

Small snapper bluefish are common throughout the coast of the Carolinas, while large chopper blues stay towards the ocean side and barrier islands. Bluefish show up in April in the Carolinas and stay until November. Their spring runs on the piers and at the beaches are lengthy.

The huge Outer Banks chopper bluefish are generally cold water fish, caught sometimes in December through April when warm winds blow through. These runs are unpredictable.

Bluefish have sharp teeth so tackle must be rugged. When fishing exclusively for bluefish wire leaders or heavy fluorocarbon or mono leaders are best. If you use wire go with black wire and dark swivels because blues will snap at anything shiny and might cut you off.

For snapper blues rods 6 6" to 9 feet and 12 lb test line and a heavy fluorocarbon or mono leader are fine. For the chopper blues and the big Outer Banks fish you need heavy tackle and wire leaders.

Fireball bottom rigs that feature red floats to attract blues work well for them. Some people think the floats keep the bait away from crabs, but blue crabs can swim so that's not true (blue crabs have been laughing about this old myth for years). Still, red attracts bluefish as well as it attracts a bull at a bullfight. Use double-hook rigs for small blues and big single float rigs for large ones. Any standard bottom rig without floats will also catch bluefish.

If pesky bait-stealers are not around the best bluefish bait is a big, juicy fresh chunk of cut bait. Mullet, menhaden (pogies), spot or fresh cut bluefish is all good. They will hit any fresh cut fish. When jumping mullet schools are present finger mullet make a great live bait for blues. Blues also hit cut shrimp, squid, and bloodworms fished on the bottom as well as artificial cut baits like Fishbites.

Catching schooling blues on lures is the thrill of an angling lifetime. In boats and on piers weighted pencil plugs like the Gotcha brand are proven winners. When using these jigging lures red headed models with white bodies are standard, but many different color combinations are available and will work. I've seen blues landed on bright pink spotted Gotcha plugs. The best retrieve is a moderately fast one with jerks and sweeps of the rod tip.

Other hard plugs, spoons and bucktails will catch bluefish. Soft plastics will also work but blues will chew them. Blues love the scented soft baits like Gulp lures, but you are going to get them chewed up. You can use short black wire or heavy fluorocarbon or mono leaders to prevent cut-offs of your lures, though heavier leaders can deter strikes. In the surf you can throw Hopkins, Sting Silver, Johnson and similar spoons. When hungry, blues will hit anything shiny or red. Even freshwater bass lures from the bottom of your tackle box may work.

Snapper bluefish go from a few ounces to a few pounds and are the best blues for eating. Larger blues have a strong flavor and are often released. The North Carolina record is a 31 lb, 12 ounce fish caught at Cape Hatteras in 1972, while the South Carolina record blue is a 21 pound fish caught in 1975 in Charleston.

6. How to Catch Spanish Mackerel

Spanish mackerel are the smaller cousins of the prized king mackerel that Carolina big game anglers target. Spanish are smaller, easier to catch, and better tasting. They don't go deep into the inlets and waterways but can be caught during the warm months in the surf, from an ocean pier, or just off the beach in a boat.

Boaters also troll for them in near-shore waters. They are a schooling fish favoring warm water and fast-moving, shiny baits.

Spanish mackerel show up in the Carolinas as the water warms from spring to summer. They are most present from June to September and favor water temperatures above 70 degrees. Anglers watch for feeding birds which move with the schools of Spanish as they cut though hapless baitfish. On fishing piers Spanish are found only at the furthest end away from the beach.

Standard 6' 6" to 8 foot rods are fine for Spanish. Use line 8 to 12 lb test with no leader if you can. Despite the fact that they are toothy many anglers prefer no leader since Spanish are a very observant, hardware-shy fish. When Spanish and blues are present that means you may have to settle for either fewer bites or some cut-offs. If you must use a leader try 20 lb monofilament or fluorocarbon instead of wire. Wire spooks Spanish.

Fishing with bait you should use around a 2/0 hook, and some anglers take them on float rigs as you would for speckled trout (only in much deeper water). Spanish can be taken by bottom fishermen with cut bait, but this is not the best way to target them.

Live baitfish like finger mullet or small bluefish will catch Spanish mackerel on the float rigs. Live shrimp works as well. They occasionally strike cut bait fished on a fireball rig like bluefish. Most surf anglers seeking Spanish throw metal lures at them, taking advantage of both the Spanish's love of flash and the casting distance of metal.

Many Spanish are caught on artificial lures. The most popular from piers are the Gotcha-style pencil plugs. Red, orange and yellow heads are popular, as are white and silver or gold bodies. You can also troll these lure in a boat. Trolling boats board a lot of Spanish.

Spanish mackerel are well known to favor shiny metal lures, and these are the biggest Spanish takers. Any kind of silver or gold spoon will work, including favorites like Hopkins, Johnson, or Kastmaster. Spoons can be cast or trolled. Spanish like a faster retrieve than even bluefish. It is sometimes hard to reel fast enough to avoid a hungry Spanish mackerel.

Most Spanish caught are a few pounds. A five pound Spanish is a notable fish. North Carolina's record is 13 lbs caught in 1987 in Ocracoke Inlet. The South Carolina record was 11 lbs caught in 1983 in Myrtle Beach. Spanish mackerel are very tasty fish, terrific grilled, broiled, or fried.

7. How to Catch Pompano

Pompano are a fun, flashy fish that are a blast to catch in the surf during the summer. Just a few tips and tricks can mean the difference between taking home a cooler full of the colorful and great-tasting fish and going home empty-handed.

Anyone drowning cut shrimp from a pier or in the surf during the summer can catch a few pompano. But to really get into some good pompano fishing you need to target them specifically and keep a few things in mind.

Pompano love sand fleas. Sand fleas (also called sand fiddlers or mole crabs) are all over the beach during the summer. They are the little crustaceans you feel moving under your feet at the edges of the surf when you are swimming at the beach. Sand fleas are the reason we have so many pompano in the summer surf. The sleek, silver fish are built to eat sand fleas, as they can even turn their streamlined bodies sideways and run into the shallowest parts of the surf to munch on them with their sharp little teeth.

If you want to catch pompano, use sand fleas. You can gather them by hand (kids are wonderful at this) or by specially made surf rakes. I can usually find enough by just grabbing for them in the sand near the piers where they like to gather.

You can impale the sand fleas on two-hook bottom rigs and cast them into and just beyond the whitewater where the pompano are waiting to inhale your bait.

Speaking of casting for pompano, remember that we aren't fishing for chopper bluefish here. You want your sand fleas right in the whitewater or just beyond it. Even big pompano will venture into the shallowest surf, turning themselves sideways to snag sand fleas. One reason sand fleas dig so fast is that they are built to avoid those hungry pompano.

If you cast as far as you can from the surf or walk way out on the pier you are going to miss most of the pompano action. Occasionally big pompano will be caught out near the ends of the piers, but this is not the regular routine and will not fill your cooler. Think shallow surf and whitewater, where the hungry pompano are feeding.

Now, about gold hooks. The rumors are true. Pompano love gold hook. Of course, if you have a tasty sand flea on the rig then pompano will hit on any kind of hook. But the shine of gold actually mimics the shine of a sand flea in the surf, which makes gold hooks more effective for pompano even if you are fishing with cut shrimp or bloodworms.

Also try to make your own rigs or buy the ones without all the snaps and swivels. Never buy wire rigs for pompano. Those rigs don't increase the bite. What will are gold hooks—and a red bead isn't a bad idea either. Some folks claim that the pregnant sand fleas that carry orange roe are a pompano's absolute favorite, and I'm not inclined to disagree.

So a red or orange bead just before the hook (just one, don't go crazy) can help you out as well. The NC tackle company Sea Striker makes great pompano rigs with gold hooks and red beads that work well and are sold at many tackle shops.

Pompano are generally a small fish under a pound. Two and three pound pompano are not uncommon, though. A four pound pompano is a trophy and the species can get even bigger. Reports of giant pompano in the Carolinas often mean a surf or pier fisherman has hooked up with a wayward permit, a more southernly fish that greatly resembles the pompano and gets huge.

Pompano are tasty at the table, in fact they are world renowned among seafood chefs. Don't fry them though…southerners love to fry fish but…just don't. Broil or bake them, or learn to cook the gourmet recipe Pompano in Papers. There are recipes for pompano later in this book.

8. How to Catch Spot

Spot are the favored saltwater panfish of the Carolinas. Unaccountably disdained by many anglers to the north and south, these small but feisty fish are a traditional target for thousands of Carolina pier and surf anglers. There is no better way of introducing a kid to saltwater fishing than by catching spot on an ocean pier.

Spot are little cousins to the larger drum family members such as redfish and speckled trout and they are very closely related to sea mullet, croaker, and silver perch. They are an important food fish in the Carolinas and when they are present can be caught in enormous numbers.

Spot are found in the surf and throughout inshore waters most of the year. They make huge runs in the spring and especially the fall, but can also be caught in smaller numbers in the summer and winter. Fall run spot tend to be larger, more numerous, and colored with yellow hues because of their hormones, hence the local name 'yellow-bellied' spot.

Spot won't go under a pier or bridge but will stay a short cast away from such structure. The reasons spot won't go under a pier are an old hotly debated Carolina tackle shop and internet forum topic. In my opinion, it is because blue crabs and big flounder love to eat spot. With those monsters waiting for you under a pier, would you venture forth if you were just a little spot? Me either.

Spot can also be targeted on open, sandy beaches and in deep holes in inlets and rivers. Surf fishermen and boaters on the cleverly named Carolina 'spot yachts'…meaning any boat that will make it into the inlets and waterways to catch them…find many spot in the fall.

If you go to a pier for spot in the fall or spring you had better go early to get a place. Spot will usually be to only one side of a pier and room will be sparse. In the spring fish the south (or west) side as the spot move up the coast. In the fall stay on the north (or east) side as the spot come back down.

Spot are bottom feeders that roam in large schools looking for small organisms, shrimps, and sea worms to eat. Light spinning gear is perfect for the pier and inshore waters, while ultra-light gear can be fun inshore and longer surf rods may be necessary for the beach. You don't need heavy gear for spot. Freshwater and light saltwater spinning rods are fine.

Use standard two or three hook bottom rigs for spot. You'll catch more if you learn how to tie your own with less swivels and snaps. One to two-ounce pyramid or bank sinkers are usually enough to hold bottom, and small hooks size 4 or 6 are just right. Spot strike hard for their size and often hook themselves. If they are there, you'll catch them.

The number one traditional bait for spot is cut live bloodworms. Due to this the price of live bloodworms has increased over the years faster than the price of gas. More recently, synthetic Fishbites brand and similar artificial bloodworms have been used to great effect by spot anglers because they work just as well and stay on the hook longer, saving you money. I highly recommend Fishbites artificial bloodworms for spot. They are available at all the piers and tackle shops now. Use a small segment, just enough to cover the hook. These synthetic baits are also harder for annoying pinfish to pick off your hook, which is a big plus.

You can get Fishbites bloodworms at most coastal tackle shops or piers and even order them at a great price from my website **Surf and Salt**.

Other solid spot baits are plain old garden-variety earthworms or pieces of fresh cut shrimp. Previously frozen shrimp are not as effective but can be used. Spot are rarely caught on other baits, although clam meat will work well, and they will occasionally strike other cut baits like squid or cut fish. Spot rarely if ever hit lures.

Unfortunately the big fall spot runs of the past haven't occurred as much in recent years. Biologists suggest that is because spot don't live long and the population surges up and down. I have always suspected that the many gill nets and trawlers allowed in the nursery areas of small panfish like spot are a big factor in their reduced numbers. That is a controversial topic, though, and not one for this book. Check out my website Surf and Salt for more on fisheries policies.

Spot average under half a pound and most are smaller. The spring spot can be large, and the fall usually boasts the biggest spot. Spot are a short-lived species and spot runs vary year to year based on many factors. Currently the Carolinas have no size or creel limits on spot. They are most often eaten dressed whole and fried, and are they are truly a delightful Carolina treat.

9. How to Catch Croaker

Croaker are a Carolina kid's favorite fish and have saved the day for many adult anglers as well. They are a relatively small (though they can go a few pounds) panfish that are commonly caught in the ocean surf, on piers, and throughout waterways, inlets, and rivers.

In recent decades the northern area of North Carolina (and especially many areas of Virginia) have become known for big croaker, while lower North Carolina and South Carolina have fewer and smaller croaker.

Croaker willingly hit all sorts of natural bait on the bottom when they are present. Some anglers disdain them as food fish, while some other rate them highly. I've always thought they were great fried up like most Carolina panfish.

Croaker roam through the inshore waters and migrate along the coast similar to spot. They swim across the beaches and throughout the waterways in big schools grubbing for food on the bottom. They can be caught throughout the fishing season in all but the coldest months, and are particularly numerous in the spring and fall.

Bottom fishing is the way to catch croaker. Use just the amount of weight you need to get to the bottom: one, two or three ounces are usually enough. Light or medium light gear (even ultra-light) can be used inshore. Catch them around piers, bridges, docks, inlet mouths, all over the Intracoastal Waterway, in the rivers, and in the ocean surf.

Croaker strike rather hard for their size but don't put up a long fight. They are a grab and run fish with a small mouth, so use small hooks and little pieces of bait. Two-hook bottom rigs with number 4 or 2 hooks are just about right.

Croaker hit any bottom bait. Choices include cut shrimp, squid, bloodworms, earthworms, clam meat, and any cut fish. Fresh bait is best but croaker will hit frozen bait, though they may tear it off the hook. You can also use the Fishbites brand and similar synthetic baits.

Croakers rarely hit lures, but big ones can occasionally be caught on small bucktails and jigs. They are sometimes taken this way by anglers fishing for gray trout (weakfish). Big ones will also sometimes surprise a flounder or trout angler by nailing a live minnow.

Croaker are fine eating cleaned and fried up in the Carolina style. Make sure you keep them on ice before they are cleaned. Be careful when cleaning them as they have surprisingly sharp gills. You need to use a glove to clean a big mess of croaker.

The North Carolina record croaker is 5 lbs caught in 1981 at Oregon Inlet. The South Carolina record croaker is 4 lbs 9 ounces caught in 1979 in Charleston.

10. How to Catch Black Drum

Black drum may be my favorite saltwater fish, although they don't get a lot of respect.

Black drum are not as famous as their high-profile cousins the red drum. They are nobody's official state fish. Few people know that black drum are found throughout the Carolinas' coast and that they can get larger than even the biggest red drum. Black drum can top 100 pounds, but smaller ones are much more common and black drum under eight pounds are the best for eating. Many anglers mistake the smaller black drum for sheepshead because at that age the two fish look very similar, both having white scales with bold black vertical stripes.

Black drum are not spectacular fighters but they are powerful and usually put a sustained pull on the line once hooked. They strike relatively softly for their size preferring to take the bait in their jaws, which contain their teeth, and grind it. The hit is light like someone plucking on a guitar string (that's what your line will feel like as it vibrates). If you catch a black drum look down into its throat at those shellfish-crushing teeth. What an amazing biological asset.

Black drum are tied to hard structure because they mainly eat shellfish. Unlike red drum they do not typically cruise the sandy beach. Black drum like inshore hard structure with strong current. Jetties, bridges, piers, and anything with barnacle-encrusted pilings are black drum territory. They also roam over oyster beds.

Big black drum often favor deep water areas under bridges and in river channels. The Intracoastal Waterway is loaded with black drum habitats as are many sounds and rivers. Black drum often feed down current of pilings during a heavy tide.

Smaller black drum can be taken on standard two-hook bottom rigs on medium-light tackle with rods 6' 6" to 8 feet with 8 to 12 lb test line. Big black drum specialists often rely on the strength of short but powerful extra-heavy rods and 20 to 25 lb test.

For smaller drum use a 2 or 3 ounce bank or other rounded sinker (pyramid sinkers hang up frequently around structure) and number 1 to 2/0 hooks. Big black drum are sought with fishfinder rigs, big barrel weights, and hooks 5/0 or larger. Currents in the deep channels where big drum lurk are strong so heavy weights and leader (but not wire) is required. You want your bait on or near the bottom as that is where black drum feed.

Some anglers prefer traditional fixed-sinker drum rigs over fishfinders. They tie their running line to one loop of a three-loop swivel, with leader line (heavy mono or fluoro-carbon) attached to one other loop and running to the hook. A snap for the sinker is attached to the third loop. I like fishfinder rigs with a sliding sinker so I can detect a black drum's soft vibrating bite.

Small black drum are taken most often on fresh cut shrimp. Many are caught incidentally by bottom anglers fishing for other species this way. Live or whole dead shrimp will work as well and you can use previously frozen bait shrimp (though fresh is better). Black drum will hit almost any natural bait on occasion, including squid, cut bait, and minnows, but they prefer shellfish and that is the way to target them. Fiddler crabs, sand fleas, cut blue crab, and clam meat are good black drum baits.

Black drum are not normally taken on lures but may hit a weighty bucktail jig if it is tipped with shrimp and fished very slowly. White and yellow are the best colors for this. They may occasionally strike synthetic shrimp-imitation baits like the Gulp or DOA brands and they hit the Fishbites synthetic baits well. I have caught many black drum in the winter on the artificial bloodworm Fishbites.

Don't ask me why as bloodworms are not the first bait you think of when black drum come up. But they hit them, I assure you. Maybe winter black drum are just plain hungry.

Black drum get huge and the biggest copper-tinged giants go into the triple digits. Big black drum are not good to eat and are often infested with many parasites. At that size black drum are actually a dull gray and all big black drum should be released.

Black drum under about eight pounds are white with big bold black stripes which fade as the fish get older. Striped black drum are delicious to eat and good in many recipes. You should still release very small drum, however.

Currently North Carolina has no size or creel limits on black drum at all but South Carolina does. In a frustrating twist, NC doesn't regulate black drum enough and the SC laws are too strict! Make sure you check the limits in SC and throw back the little ones everywhere.

11. How to Catch Sea Mullet

Sea mullet, also called whiting, Virginia mullet, roundheads, and kingfish, are an important food and small game species along the Atlantic Coast and Gulf of Mexico. There are three different species that overlap in the Carolinas; all look similar and are caught by identical methods.

Anglers often refer to whiting as sea mullet or just mullet even though they are not related to real mullet like the striped mullet. Whiting are instead members of the drum family and close cousins to spot, croaker, redfish, and sea trout.

Sea mullet do not get very large but are highly valued as a tasty panfish and they put up a short but spirited fight for their size. Sea mullet strike hard trying to grab you bait and run off with it. They are commonly caught from the surf or ocean piers but will also enter inshore waters.

Sea mullet are around most of the fishing season with the exception of the coldest months. The Carolinas sometimes have runs of winter whiting on the piers as early as February and as late as December, if any piers are open. Early spring sea mullet action is often the best thing going in the surf in relatively cold temperatures.

The surf just behind the breakers is one of the best places to find sea mullet. They like to eat sand fleas and other small shellfish which they suck up with their small mouths like a vacuum cleaner. You can also look for holes in the surf (called sloughs, pronounced slews) where deep water exists and draws both shellfish and sea mullet.

Whiting run in small pods but not in huge schools like croaker or spot. If they are there they will often provide steady action while the tide is moving. They often stage nice runs at night or when the tide is running heavily. Some anglers claim a strong wind helps a sea mullet bite.

Most sea mullet rigs feature two-hook rigs with size 4 or 6 hooks and two-ounce pyramid or bank sinkers. Use as little weight as you can to reach the bottom. They are a fish of the sea floor with an underslung mouth so make sure you are fishing on the bottom. Rods 6' 6" to 8 feet are fine while surf fishermen may need a longer 9 or 10-foot rod to reach whiting out behind a sand bar.

Sea mullet love fresh cut shrimp. They also bite squid and bloodworms reliably. Earthworms will work as will cut bait. Sand fleas can be used the same way they are used for pompano. Remember, use a small piece of bait as whiting are a grab and run fish. Very large whiting can be taken on small jigs bounced on the bottom.

Whiting range from tiny to about two pounds, though slightly larger ones are caught all the time. Because of their torpedo-like body they can be filleted, but most folks fry or bake them whole and dressed. Sea mullet are among the best tasting fish of the Carolinas.

12. How to Catch Sheepshead

Sheepshead are a Carolina inshore saltwater fish that is popular among anglers who like to fish for them and popular with seafood lovers who like to eat them. Sheepshead at one time spread as far north as New York where Sheepshead Bay near Coney Island was named for them. In recent decades, however, they have been regarded as a southern fish with most catches coming south of Virginia along the south Atlantic and Gulf Coasts.

Sheepshead average about three pounds but can get over ten, and are terrific fighters who like to run anglers' lines around the pilings where they are most often caught. Their bite is very hard to detect and they are a difficult fish to hook if you don't know what you are doing. The fish gets its name from its sheep-like lips that probe pilings for barnacles, mussels, and other shellfish.

Sheepshead are tied to hard structure such as bridges, jetties, docks, and piers. They use their sharp teeth to scrap barnacles from this structure and gobble up and break the shells of barnacles, mussels, and crabs. They do not travel in schools but orientate themselves around a food source and become very territorial, often staying in an area until the food supply is used up. They are tolerant of temperature extremes and can be found in all but the coldest or hottest weather within their range.

Catching sheepshead is not easy. They are sometimes caught incidentally by bottom fishermen using shrimp for bait and are intentionally hooked and fought by some crafty Carolina anglers who target them. A strong rod and heavier than usual line, around 20 lb test, is recommended when fishing for them as sheepshead quickly try to run when hooked and wrap your line around those pilings. It is important to put strong pressure on the fish to bring them away from the hang-ups.

Sheepshead are caught on unusual saltwater baits and rarely take usual ones such as bloodworms, squid or cut fish. Instead they hit fiddler crabs, pieces of larger crabs such as cut blue crab, sand fleas (also called mole crabs) or even barnacles scrapped from a piling and held together by their own sticky mesh or rubber bands.

Despite their brute strength sheepshead have a bite that it is so soft it is often impossible to detect. The old saying among sheepshead fishermen is that you must set the hook just before a sheepshead hits! It's not really that difficult…but it almost is. One trick is to watch the rod tip, which will have a slight dip from the weight of your sinker. When a sheepshead bites the dip will disappear as the tip rises. Even if you feel nothing, set the hook. Really, if you have any suspicions at all, set the hook.

Sheepshead anglers don't stay in one place but move from piling to piling. Sometimes sheepshead can be seen in clear water rising up and slowly working on the barnacles and mussels of the pilings. All sheepshead have those pro-truding lips that give the fish its name. They also have a white body and big, black bold stripes. They are sometimes confused with black drum, another inshore structure fish that covers the same areas but is easier to catch.

Sheepshead are a hearty, tasty fish that yield delicious white meat fillets which fit into many seafood recipes. Sheepshead fillets are also very good simply breaded and fried.

13. A Carolina Angler's Guide to Inshore Scented Soft Baits

Winter in the Carolinas is a great time for boat shows and tackle expos, and if you go to one you will see a bewildering selection of lures available for throwing at inshore saltwater fish. The Bass Pro Shops, Dick's Sporting Goods, all of our fine local coastal tackle shops, and even the Walmarts carry tons of artificial lure choices today. All of them work in the right situation, and you shouldn't be reluctant to try some of the newer models out there gaining fame for their success.

As far as shallow-water fishing goes, most of the saltwater lures available are targeted toward two species: speckled trout and redfish. You will also find lures and rigs meant for flounder, bluefish, pompano and other species, but the bulk of the stuff out there is geared at specks and reds. In recent years, however, even tackle intended for little saltwater panfish like spot and croaker has gained space in the tackle shops.

The biggest innovation of the past decade in angling has been the rise of synthetic baits meant to feel and smell just like the real thing. Lifelike lures made with natural ingredients that dispense fish-attracting scent into the water exploded on the scene a while back and now everyone uses them. That is because where once scented lures were a con, today's synthetic soft baits really work.

A lot of good companies make a lot of good lures when it comes to inshore fishing, but the line that gets the most attention in the Carolinas these days is the Gulp lures manufactured by Berkley out of Iowa. Gulps come in a lot of shapes, colors and sizes, but their main attraction is their scent, which at times allows them to out-fish even wriggling live bait. A product that was years in the development, Gulp soft baits (which actually contain no plastic) disperse scent as soon as they hit the water, attracting fish and making them hang onto the lure for the extra few seconds needed to set the hook.

Since they became an overnight sensation, Berkley Gulps have developed a cult following, including many devoted speckled trout anglers and top fishing guides. Because Gulps come in many different molds and sizes, each fan seems to have their favorite can't miss choice.

Popular styles of Gulp lures include swimming minnow and mullet models, straight jerk shad bodies, fluke bodies, more traditional looking grubs and shrimp-imitating tails. There are lots of different colors to choose, with pearl white, chartreuse, new penny, pink and the infamous electric (or nuclear) chicken being top sellers. Gulp lures for specks and redfish are usually from 3 to 5 inches and can be rigged on jig heads or in various other ways, including free-lining.

Many other companies besides Gulp have gotten into the scent-dispersal game. The age-old debate about whether fish smell lures seems to have been settled, as products that contain scent are huge sellers and they produce. Many of the new synthetic lures have bodies that resemble shrimp, which is the main food in the diet of a speckled trout and is also eaten by about everything else that swims in the Carolina waters.

One of the biggest sellers of imitation shrimp lures is the DOA brand out of Stuart, Florida. DOA shrimp, as well as the many other shrimp-imitating brands out there such as the popular Billy Bay Halo Shrimp, have the look and feel of the real thing. You can fish them on a jig head or weight-less, while some models have a small weight built into the body. They work just like live shrimp under a popping cork or float rig. There are also weedless models of these imita-tion shrimp, which are effective when throwing into marsh grass or around hard structure.

These soft-bodied baits are great choices for trout and redfish, and will often outfish traditional lures like plastic grubs and hard plugs. They will even beat live bait on occa-sion. In the middle of winter, when live bait is nearly impos-sible to come by, such lures are invaluable. Speaking of value, these lures are not exactly cheap, so throwing them into a mess of underwater structure is always a risky propo-sition.

When fishing these soft lures, you usually want to fish pretty slowly, with frequent pauses to let your target zero in on the scent. Use as little weight as you need to get the lure to where the fish are feeding. I really like a pull-and-pause method very similar to the way we all learned to fish plastic worms for bass on those long-ago farm ponds. Lures like these are often hit on the fall, or even when sitting still or rolling with the tide.

These days there are also body patterns meant to re-semble things other than shrimp and minnows. Crab-like bodies are popular with drum fishermen, while there are imitation sand flea baits that appeal to pompano, sea mullet, and sheepshead.

Our Carolina panfish are not left out the scent-revolution. Several years ago the company Fishbites out of St. Augustine, Florida began marketing synthetic alternatives to fresh cut bait, which can be added to the hooks of small-bottom rigs. There are flavors of shrimp and squid, but the most successful flavor has been the 'Bag O Worms' baits, which are bloodworm alternatives.

Bloodworms have always been the best bait for spot, the most popular panfish of the Carolinas. I have always found their price per bag rather unreasonable. These prices seem to mysteriously spike when the spot are running in the fall. Bloodworm bits are easily torn off the hook as well and rarely last past one caught spot (or one hungry uncaught pinfish). The Fishbites bloodworms save you money, since they are held on by tough mesh and will stay on the hook for several caught fish as well as resisting the nibbling pinfish longer.

When it comes to all these new synthetic soft baits, don't get me wrong. The more traditional lures made of plastic, as well as plain old live and natural baits, are still just fine for filling your cooler. Sometimes fish want live bait and won't take anything else. If you haven't tried the newer scented lures however, you should give them a shot. Change can be good, and a few speckled trout or frisky redfish on the line will persuade even the most dyed-in-the-wool traditionalists to give scientific progress a shot.

14. A Guide to Carolina Fishing Rigs

The best rule when using a rig for cut bait or live bait fishing is 'the simpler the better.' The less hardware like snaps and swivels you have lying on the bottom or moving through the water column the better. Don't go for the flash that is meant to attract fishermen and not fish. Simple rigs catch fish.

If you can learn to tie your own fishing rigs without all the extra swivels and snaps you'll have an advantage since they work better than most store-bought rigs.

However, the Morehead City, North Carolina tackle company Sea Striker sells some great pre-tied rigs that have fewer bells and whistles. If you can't tie your own bottom rigs seek out the Sea Striker brands. They come in small packages marketed for pompano, drum, flounder, sea mullet, croaker, spot and other inshore fish.

You can also find some pre-tied rigs in the better tackle shops that don't use all the snaps and tied simply by veteran bottom fishermen who know what they are doing.

Here are the main rigs used in surf and pier fishing and inshore saltwater fishing:

High-low bottom rig

This is the standard rig sold in all the tackle and pier shops. It consists of two or three hooks positioned above a clip for a sinker at the bottom. For saltwater panfish you need hook sizes 4 or 6, for larger bluefish or red drum you want to go with a bigger hook around 1/0. Usually you add standard J-hooks to this rig.

Sinker sizes usually range from 1 to 4 ounces, with 2 ounce being the standard size from the pier and surf fishermen sometimes using a lot of lead to get the rig out there. You usually use pyramid or bank sinkers with these rigs.

Fishfinder rig

This is my favorite rig, the best one to use with live bait when fishing on the bottom. The idea behind a fishfinder rig is to let the weight sit on the bottom while the live bait moves about on its own, reacting to the presence of nearby predator fish.

Trolling or drifting the fishfinder rig isn't any better than a fixed-sinker rig like a high-low rig, but when casting it allows you to know exactly what is going on at the terminal end of your rig, since the weight sits on the bottom and you can feel the live bait moving. It is great for feeling flounder bites, since they tend to take the live bait in their mouth and you don't usually hit a flounder right away. The same thing applies to sheepshead and black drum. In freshwater Carolina anglers targeting catfish use this rig to great effect.

To make a fishfinder rig you first thread an egg sinker to the line running from the rod and reel. Go with the smallest sinker you can get away with, but remember you have to get the rig down to the bottom. One ounce is common, and you can go heavier in heavy current.

After threading on the egg sinker, tie on a black barrel swivel which serves as the stopper for the egg sinker. Use black so bluefish won't bite at your swivel. To the other free loop of the swivel you tie on about 15 inches of leader material. I like 20 lb monofilament test in most situations, but you can use whatever strength you like or use fluorocarbon leader. Stay away from wire leader unless you are after big bluefish or sharks, as wire reduces bites.

You can also use a pyramid, bell, bank or other sinker if you also use one small bead (usually red) between the sinker and the swivel to stop the weight. At the end of your rig you simply tie on your hook. Kahle-style curved hooks or circle hooks work well with live bait, but any kind of hook can go at the end of a fishfinder rig.

Float rig

A float rig can be used from the pier, shore or boat...although it is usually not used in the surf. It is a favored rig for speckled trout anglers fishing live shrimp. It has a few variations but is basically just a float (often a popping cork) above a weight, a length of leader, and a hook. Most speckled trout anglers use slip floats so they can adjust the depth of their bait as they find out where the fish are holding in the water column. At times just a split shot or two will do as weight, while in heavy current you may need to use an egg sinker on a float rig.

In addition to speckled trout, float rigs are also used for redfish, flounder (in shallow water), black drum, sheepshead, bluefish, and even Spanish mackerel. Some anglers use a treble hook at the end of a float rig but that makes taking fish off the hook harder and may kill an undersized fish, so I prefer circle hooks on float rigs. Just remember you don't have to set the hook using circle hooks, just play the fish.

15. Using MirrOlures to Catch Speckled Trout and Redfish

MirrOlures are a flashy type of saltwater plug that has been manufactured by L&S Bait Company out of Florida for decades. They have only improved over the years and are terrific inshore plugs to use when targeting speckled trout and redfish. The flash of a MirrOlure in the water imitates baitfish like mullet on which trout and redfish heavily feed. MirrOlures have great casting weight which allows anglers to throw them long distances and even makes them a good weapon for surf anglers seeking trout and redfish.

Classic MirrOlure plugs such as the 52MR, the TTM, and the 7M dive a few feet and are perfect for shallow and medium action. One key is to fish these MirrOlures slowly as they were designed to be fished. Anglers can use a pull and pause technique or fish the Mirrolure as a twitchbait, but you should make the retrieve relatively slow compared to retrieves used when fishing for bluefish or Spanish mackerel.

MirrOlure also now makes some popular topwater models which work great when the speckled trout bite is on in the morning. The MirrOlure TopDog and the smaller, popular SheDog are great MirrOlures to use as topwater targets, retrieving the plug in a side-to-side 'walk the dog' method.

The SheDog also has sonic attributes as it rattles and will bring speckled trout and redfish from a distance. The SheDog MirrOlure is a great lure to use in tainted or choppy water.

These are the Mirrolure plugs that most inshore salt-water anglers are familiar with. They are the classic lure for speckled trout fishing. There are shallow, medium and deep-diving plugs in this group:

MirrOlure Model TTM - 3-5/8"; 1/2 oz; dives 1'-4'
MirrOlure Model 52MR - 3-5/8";1/2 oz; dives 3'-5'
MirrOlure Model 7M - 3-5/8"; 3/8 oz; dives 0'-6'
MirrOlure Model 77M - 4-1/4"; 1-1/4 oz; dives 5'-10'
MirrOlure Model 65M - 3-1/4"; 1 oz; dives 10'-20'

Remember, MirrOlures are often best fished with a pull and pause method which imitates a live baitfish. When you look at a baitfish like a mullet in the water you don't see them speeding in a straight line. Instead they are darting side to side, pushing forward and pausing, as they fight against the current or try to make themselves bad targets for preda-tory fish, crabs, and birds. You want your lure to move along the same way. Fish like speckled trout often favor a relatively slow retrieve.

In hotter water when fish are very active you can fish MirrOlures as a twitchbait, throwing in jerks and jabs as you retrieve. You still don't want to go too fast. The strong pull of a redfish as it hits a MirrOlure is an exhilarating experi-ence.

MirrOlure Topwater Lure

The new Top Dog is MirrOlure's answer to anglers' requests for a topwater jerkbait plug from the company. This is the perfect bait for fishing schooling speckled trout, redfish or bluefish that are hitting on top. It has an under-chin tie-in point so you can use the 'walk the dog' topwater retrieve that really turns trout and redfish on.

To use the 'walk the dog' technique retrieve the plug in a side-to-side motion. The topwater bait will cause a commotion on the surface which can attract trout or redfish from a great distance.

16. Tips for Targeting Big Doormat Flounder

Quite a few traditional Carolina flounder fishermen are content to drift or troll the inlets dragging live bait on the bottom and letting the boat do the work for them. But for those anglers seeking larger flatfish, anchoring up and casting to structure is a better tactic. With size limits increasing every year more and more anglers are using tactics that target big doormat flounder.

Big flounder love to orientate themselves around hard structure inshore. Docks, bridges, piers, jetties, and oyster beds near marsh grass are great places to find them. These larger female fish are a bit lazier than their smaller male cousins and prefer to lie in wait around some sort of baitfish-attracting structure (like pilings or rocks) that will bring a steady flow of straggling small fish (mullet, pogies, spot, croaker, pinfish, etc) when the tide really starts moving either in or out.

Here are some tips for catching these larger flounder:

Anchor up and cast

Stop drifting around and anchor up near likely floun-der spots. Work areas completely and thoroughly when the tide is moving using either live bait or scented soft baits. Cast into structure and let the tide do some of the work for you. Use short hops off the bottom and don't be hesitant to crawl the bait or lure and use frequent pauses.

If you are using live bait you'll need to give the floun-der some time to take the bait. If you opt for lures set the hook immediately upon the strike, except with the scented soft baits. You should give flounder a few seconds with those.

What's a good live bait rig for big flounder?

A simple fishfinder rig will do best and hang up less. Thread an egg sinker onto your running line. Use as little weight as you can, but you must be on the bottom for floun-der so anything between 1 to 3 ounces is possible depending on the current. 1 ounce is usually a good starting point.

After you thread on the sinker tie on a swivel. To the other end attach your leader. I use 20 or 25 lb mono line and never get bite-offs from flounder. Other anglers and guides prefer different leader material, though. Don't use a leader that is too heavy and don't use wire leader. After 15 to 22 inches of leader tie on the hook, something like a 1/0 or 2/0 Kahle hook or a circle hook.

Hook mud minnows through the lips and finger mullet through the eye sockets. This rig works terrific with any of the other baitfish, plus small crabs or live shrimp.

Can I really catch big flounder on lures around structure?

You absolutely can, and it is one of the best ways. You don't have to drift the day away. You can work faster and cover more territory by anchoring or using a trolling motor around docks and other structure and throwing live bait or lures.

Flounder love to hit today's scented soft baits. Use a lead head jig of ¼ or 3/8 ounce depending on the current (jig head size varies based on how strong the tide is) and make sure you can make contact with the bottom. Then add the scented soft bait of your choice. There are plenty of strip baits marketed just for flounder now, although fluke and shad bodies that are often used for trout and redfish can be deadly on big flounder as well.

Gulp and Fishbites make great scented soft baits for flounder fishing, as do other companies out there. Remember to fish them slowly and keep the lure falling back to the bottom. Most successful anglers like to hop the lures a little then let them pause as they fall back like a struggling baitfish. You can also use a slow, steady crawl. Flounder will really pounce on these scented baits as they rise up from around structure.

17. Winter Saltwater Fishing in the Carolinas

Carolina winters can be mild or unusually harsh. Despite what most people think, there is usually something biting on the Carolina coast no matter how cold it gets. Winter fishing can be a lonely but rewarding experience.

For the casual bottom angler and the surf fishermen there are targets out there, though they might not be easy to find. Fish are schooled up tight, meaning it isn't hard to miss out on them if you are at the wrong spot at the wrong time. Some of them also tend to be more active at certain times of the day and night.

Among these bottom fish are red and black drum, silver perch and spot. All of them can be caught on simple cut shrimp, which is easy to fish in the winter because the bothersome little pinfish have sought warmer waters. Winter fish are usually active only on moving tides and far more likely to be found around hard structure such as piers, bridges and docks than on sandy stretches of beach.

Black drum orient themselves to places where shell-fish cling, and nice-sized fish perfect for filleting can be caught throughout the winter into spring. Despite the chill, black drum will hit better at night. During the day you might not know they are there.

Many more people fish for speckled trout or redfish than for black drum in the colder months, and these anglers often take a ride out to the jetties for trout or target huge schools of reds in shallow water and back creeks. Experienced locals have a strong advantage in the winter since finding the fish is the key: location is everything. You don't want to waste a lot of time riding around from place to place in the cold if you aren't catching fish.

Trout and redfish anglers will mostly be throwing lures, probably including some they got for Christmas. Fishing these lures this time of the year is an exercise in patience. If you cast them out and retrieve them quickly, as you might in warmer seasons, you won't be bothered by the annoyance of netting fish into the boat. You have to fish very slowly.

Even predatory game fish will not expending much energy chasing down prey in cold water, they will hover around spots where food will be brought to them by the current. They won't chase down your lure even if you're sitting right on a school. It takes a great deal of patience to slow down and fish correctly, as most of the hits will happen when the lure is falling slowly back or sitting still.

Unlike black drum, there will be some days when lethargic trout and redfish won't hit until the sun warms things up a little bit. They'll be feeding on minnows, shrimp and crabs and hitting lures that imitate these baits.

Today's trout and redfish lures are perfectly suited to the winter months, as brands like the Gulp line of baits and the various shrimp imitation lures add lifelike feel and scent to traditional patterns. Since the movement of the lure plays a far less important role in cold weather, feel and smell are crucial.

Other critters are abroad in the winter as well. Pelicans and other birds will be feeding on minnows in the clear cold water, while dolphins will seek out redfish of their own to eat. Skates, rays and small sharks may hit your bottom baits in the surf or around the bridges. Skates are especially hardy and are out there all through the winter.

Game and food fish are out there too, but it takes some of your own hardiness and dedication to find them. If you do start catching fish, remember they are schooled up tight and likely to be concentrated in a small place, at least while a running tide lasts. Whether it is trout and redfish on warmer days or black drum on cold nights, bringing back a fresh fish dinner during a cold Carolina winter is still a possibility.

18. Dark Secrets: Night Fishing in the Carolinas

Angling after dark is actually a fun and productive way to fish and it has several advantages over fishing during the daytime. There are quite a few reasons to wait and focus your efforts until after the sun goes down.

Night fishing gets you out of the sun

The obvious reason to fish at night is to get out of the sun's bright rays, and night fishing can be a relaxing and enjoyable way to continue fishing in the summer when the heat has become just too much to bear. This is actually healthier for you anyway, since the sun's rays damage the skin.

One warning: although you won't need sunscreen, don't forget that mosquitoes are more active at night so you still need to pack bug spray.

You can escape the crowds by fishing at night

Summertime at the pier or boat ramp can be maddeningly crowded as fishermen crawl all over each other to get a line in the water. Summer means a mix of local and vacationing anglers and is the busiest time on the waterways and on the roads to get to the fishing hole.

If you fish at night, though, you can often find yourself wonderfully isolated. Most anglers fish during the day, so night fishing is a time when you can get back some of the best joys of angling: quiet solitude and peaceful co-existence with nature. You also get your choice of fishing spots, which is a blessing in these days of user conflict over access.

Night fishing is actually best for some fish species

There are fish who hit better at night regardless of what season it is. These are fish that anglers target at night for more reasons than to beat the heat.

In freshwater, catfish are well-known as nocturnal feeders that really go on the prowl after dark. Since catfish feed more by smell than by sight they are the prefect nighttime predators, and they can sense bait from a great distance. Anyone who targets catfish knows they hit better at night, and many dedicated catfish pros won't get on the water until the sun goes down.

For a Carolina inshore angler, drum are the equivalent of catfish, really coming alive at night. Both redfish and black drum hit better at night, with redfish prowling the surf and the creek mouths for prey and black drum hanging around bridges, piers, and docks feeding on shellfish. Black drum in particular are like catfish, feeding more by smell than sight and zeroing in on shellfish. They even have chin barbells which function much like the whiskers on catfish.

One question: can fish see at night?

Yes they can, so don't worry about your favorite fish species. Redfish, speckled trout, flounder and other predator fish feed at night nearly as much as they do during the day, especially during fuller moons. Many people wonder if fish can see their lures and baits after dark, and the answer is that they can. A phosphorous glow colors baits and lures in the water at night, meaning fish looking up into the moonlight can see your bait just fine.

Take a tip from me and give night fishing a try. It is a relaxing and fun way to escape the heat and the crowds and get back to what fishing is all about: you, nature, and a lot of fish on the line.

19. Tips for Catching Live Bait

Finding and catching your own live bait can be one of the biggest joys of saltwater fishing. Live bait can be a key to catching game fish like speckled trout, redfish, flounder and bluefish. Since bait choices are many and diverse inshore saltwater anglers have lots of opportunities to do the go-it-yourself route as opposed to buying live bait.

One important bait gathering step is to buy a cast net. Whether you fish from pier, shore or small boat, cast nets are wonderful bait-catching devices that pay for themselves many times over. Don't buy a bigger net than you can throw. A cast net is measured by its radius, and a five-foot net is plenty big enough for most folks.

Cast nets allow you to encircle such quick prey as finger mullet and live shrimp. Finger mullet, running around in schools that can seem deceptively small when they're leaping out of the water, are a terrific bait for flounder, bluefish and redfish. Live shrimp are the absolute premier bait for speckled trout.

You will also find small pinfish if you use a cast net for long. Little pinfish are a neat secret weapon that will nab some nice flounder and big cruising speckled trout for you. Large ones can be cut up for strip bait.

In fact, it's likely that just about anything you catch in your cast net is being eaten by something worth catching in the area. Sometimes what you net tells you what to fish. Just make sure not to throw your cast net over rocks or oyster shells, or you'll have to buy a new one.

There are other simple ways of gathering bait if you can't throw a cast net. A well-laid minnow trap will yield results if baited and left long enough. This method will in particular gather mud minnows, a diverse species of small killifish that are top baits for flounder on bottom rigs. Small tiger-sided and striped killifish are among the hardiest minnows available for flounder fishing, if you can capture some. They are very active on the hook and flounder love them.

Of course, there is also the do-it-by-hand method of gathering live bait. Many saltwater baits are literally there for the taking.

Fiddler crabs scurry around the mud and sand flats of sounds and waterways. Fiddler crabs are easily gathered as even the males with the big claws have a pinch that doesn't really hurt. Fiddler crabs are great bait for sheepshead and black drum when fished against structure. They will also catch some flounder from time to time.

Blue crabs can be used as well, but take care in harvesting them as their pinchers certainly do hurt. Also obey regulations since blue crabs often have size limits. Cut or halved blue crab is an unusual but highly effective bait for red and black drum often used by fishing guides when nothing else is working.

Ocean-side sand fleas (also called mole crabs) are another fantastic bait you can just gather yourself, digging them up as the whitewater rushes back into the sea. Kids love digging up sand fleas with their hands. Sand fleas make a great bait for pompano right there in the ocean surf, and also take sea mullet, sheepshead, black drum and flounder.

You can also dig up live clams in many places and use the meat as bait for saltwater panfish, black drum, and redfish.

There are many bait-gathering rigs available that you can use from a pier or a boat to catch small fish on little hooks. These are often called sabiki rigs and are jigged up and down to catch small fish to use as bait. Jig them around the pilings and you'll be surprised at how much bait you gather up.

One often overlooked but very simple saltwater bait-gathering opportunity is digging up earthworms. Earthworms are usually associated with freshwater fishing but are a great bait for many saltwater fish including croaker, spot, sea mullet, and even redfish.

No matter which method you choose it is simple and easy to gather up live bait for saltwater fishing and it will save you some money if you get proficient at it. It's also a lot of fun.

20. Using Tandem Rigs for Spring Trout and Summer Shad

Carolina anglers often have to contend with instability when fishing in the spring, from the weather to which fish will bite on a given day. That is one reason people talk about runs of fish, though in all my years I have never seen a fish run. The fish are like the changing Carolina weather: here one hour and gone the next.

Spring also finds a great variety and size of fish swimming in our inshore waters. It is possible to find the same species of fish in the same place two days in a row but encounter a much smaller (or if you're lucky, larger) version the second time. Speckled trout and bluefish, for example, are 'running' around in all different sizes in the spring.

Trout anglers in particular are often left unsure, not of just whether or not their target will hit but what size fish they will encounter and when. That is why I often tell people to tie a trailer jig on when going after trout with lures in the spring. A rig with two lures on it, one large and one small, will prepare you for what's out there and often let you know the size of the fish in local waters.

Lots of people use a jig and grub combination to fish for trout, but you can add a second jig easily to make it a tandem rig. This is a very simple thing, usually just one big jig at the front and a very small one at the back. For trout you can often just tie the rig on without a leader, although if blues are around they will cut a leaderless rig or eat your jigs in a hurry.

This kind of rig starts with a big jig head. Red is common, but trout anglers know to vary colors if things aren't working. I most often use a 3/8 ounce jig, but in rough conditions or deep water a ¼ ounce may be used. The jig is tied on the line using a couple of simple overhand loops, and about 14 to 18 inches of tag end is left hanging. To that is attached a very little jig, like you might use on freshwater crappie. This jig ends the rig.

You can use any of the popular makes and models of grubs you like on the jigs, as the grubs come in every scent and fashion these days. When I started out making this rig years ago I would just use two regular green twist-tail grubs (one large, one small) and that still works fine. The first one is usually a 3 or 4-inch grub and the second just a little crappie grub.

These days scented soft baits are so effective that tandem rigs can be even more deadly. There is no limit to the styles of grubs and colors you can mix and match on this simple rig, and it is easy just to change tails. Speckled trout are notoriously fickle so fishermen change colors often if they aren't having success. Sometimes trout even change what they want to hit within a given day.

The biggest surprise for many people is that most of the trout you catch will come on the trailing jig. Folks are always surprised to see a nice speck caught on what is essentially a crappie jig. The bigger trout often hit the bigger jig, of course, but often a nice one will wallop the little jig too. You may occasionally get two at a time.

I think the rig works so well because the first jig gets noticed, then the predator seizes on the small, easy meal behind it. I can't prove that, but it makes since to me, and there are times the rig does out-fish the heck out of people just using a single grub.

Tandem rigs with small jigs will also catch any shad that are around. Some folks don't think of shad as a saltwater fish but I have caught them in bunches off of the southeastern NC piers at times on tandem jig rigs. Shad are also caught by Carolina anglers in 'sweetwater' rivers where the water runs from salt to fresh.

American and Hickory shad make big spawning runs upstream in the Carolinas, usually around late May. During this time they will hit small jigs, especially on tandem rigs, and they put up quite a fight. Shad strike very small jigs (sometimes called darts) that are 1/16 or 1/32 ounce lures.

Pre-tied shad tandem rigs are marketed by the NC tackle company Betts and sold at fresh and saltwater tackle shops as 'spec rigs.' I've never known what the 'spec' originally was in the rig as it could have referred to speckled trout, crappie, or shad (which often have a dark spot) all of which will hit the rig. The best colors are often yellow, chartreuse, red and white, green, orange or even pink.

Shad have an interesting bone structure that makes them hard to clean (you have to know what you are doing) and some anglers throw them back, but there are traditional recipes for shad that go back many generations in the Carolinas.

21. Saltwater Tactics: Trolling for Flounder Against the Tide

Ask most Carolina anglers how to catch flounder and they will tell you to drift. From early spring through late fall our inshore waters contain a glut of boats filled with flounder fishermen drifting along with the tide. However, not every expert agrees that drifting is the best way to target the tasty flatfish.

Captain Bobby White has over 30 years of experience fishing the waters of southeastern North Carolina. He is a former fishing guide who prefers slow trolling instead of drifting when it comes to flounder.

"My father happened to be one of the best flounder fisherman in this part of the country," says White, "and he taught me a lot of things about catching those flat critters. One of the most special techniques was how to catch them while slow trolling in a boat."

White says that using your trolling motor gives you more options and lets you cover more water than just letting the current do the work.

"I believe trolling is more effective than drifting because you can control your speed and where you are going," he says. "Trolling works extremely well in those shallow and narrow creeks where you can't easily set up a drift. Trolling parallel along the backside of a sand bar along the drop off can be very effective. You can't do that drifting."

Everyone knows flounder like moving baits, but White says that the direction and speed the bait moves is of more importance than people think.

"Trolling against the current is the only way to go," he says. "Go very slow. That is the major advantage of trolling. You are going against the tide and you can really slow down."

White lets his flounder rigs trail the boat, using a one ounce sinker to hold them down.

"You must maintain contact with the bottom," he says. "Usually a one ounce weight is enough. If not, the current is too strong or the water is too deep. Depths of four feet or less are the most productive areas for flounder while trolling."

Although White ties his own flounder rigs-- complete with yellow floats, spinners, and gold hooks-- he says the rig is less important than the technique.

"You can use most any type of flounder rig when you do this," he says. "When a flounder hits a bait while trolled the rod will start to bend more than normal, just like the bottom contours produce. The difference is the rod tip will stay bent and not bounce back."

One area in which White agrees with other anglers is in giving the fish a little time to take the bait.

"Flounder are notorious for grabbing hold of the back of a minnow and hanging on," he says, "so you do have to give it a little time. They will eventually move up the min-now and encounter the hook."

White says to give the fish a few moments, but not to wait too long before setting the hook.

"Waiting too long can produce a lot of gut hooked short flounder and we don't want that," he says. "I would rather lose a few to the short strike instead of killing a bunch of juvenile flounder. Also, the bigger fish will usually get to the hook quicker anyway."

White says that the key is to make sure you are trolling slow enough.

"If you think you are going to fast you probably are," he says. "A trolling plate on your motor is the best idea, but if you don't want to do that just carry along a five gallon bucket with some holes in it, tie it to a cleat, and throw it out back. I have used two buckets before when the tide was slack."

White says that trolling may not produce the biggest doormats every time, but beats any other method for num-bers.

"Trolling for flounder is not the technique you should use for targeting citation fish," he says. "But it is the most effective way to fish the creeks for numbers. If you want a few for dinner, this is the best way to get them."

22. Saltwater Tips: Catching Spring Redfish

Fishermen in the Carolinas can get into some great redfish action during the spring provided they know a few tips and tactics. Redfish are a powerful fish that provide terrific sport for inshore anglers.

Redfish hit all kinds of lures and baits but anglers specifically targeting redfish (also called spottail bass, channel bass, red drum and puppy drum in some areas) can use several specific techniques to put more of the copper brutes into the boat or cooler.

Bottom fishing for redfish

Redfish often feed on the bottom in heavy current, near docks and rocks, and off of jetties and other structure. They stick their noses in the mud to root out shellfish and buried mud minnows, and sometimes anglers can see them around shallow areas like creeks tailing with their tails sticking up out of the water.

Fishermen can use a fishfinder rig to bottom fish for these redfish with a small stretch (about 14 to 16 inches) of monofilament line as leader. On most inshore waters a 1-ounce egg weight is usually heavy enough to get to the bottom, although in some heavy current more may be needed.

Just thread on the sinker and tie on a swivel. Attach 16 inches of monofilament leader (20 lb test line is good) and tie on the hook. Curved Kahle-style hooks or circle hooks are favorites. The fishfinder rig allows an angler to maintain contact with the bait and feel the bite without the weight of the sinker.

The best live bottom baits for redfish are small minnows like mud minnows, pogies (menhaden), or finger mullet. You can also use live shrimp, live pinfish, and small crabs. Top cut baits are mullet, spot, and blue crab. Cut shrimp will work, especially if it is fresh, as will squid and bloodworms or earthworms.

Casting jerkbaits for redfish

Jerkbaits are a type of hard lure that is a great plug for schooling redfish. They cast well, have a lot of action, and hungry redfish love to hit them hard. You can work the top, middle or bottom of the water column with these lures. When redfish are schooling up and hitting minnows in a reaction strike they will smash jerkbaits slashed through the water.

Top jerkbaits include the MirrOlure models and the many Rapal and Rat-L-Trap type plugs. Many hard jerkbaits that were traditional for largemouth bass fishermen have crossed over for use on redfish in saltwater.

Casting lead head jigs for redfish

Lead head jigs are a great way to reach spring schools of redfish. Lead heads up to 3/8 ounces are popular depending on the depth of water and the strength of current. Lead heads painted red, black, white, and yellow are popular with redfish anglers. Very popular plastic grubs to use with jig heads are the fluke, troutkiller, and long shad-tail models. Grubs in white, pearl white, chartreuse, green and clear with sparkle flakes are all popular. An angler fishes these long grubs just like the hard plug jerkbaits, working them off the bottom and giving them a slashing action which flashes to bring in the redfish.

Curly-tailed jigs in white and chartreuse are also great for catching schooling redfish. You can work curly-tailed grubs with a steadier retrieve than straight grubs because the tail gives these lures more action. You can also use a pull and pause when fishing a jig and grub which allows the lure to slowly fall back. Redfish will hit the grub during the pause as it falls. As I've noted before in this book the scented soft baits grubs like Gulp, Fishbites, and DOA brands are very popular with redfish anglers because the drum are attracted to them by smell and hold onto them longer.

Spoons

Spring redfish hit spoons such as the Kastmaster and Hopkins brands and also the many styles of weedless spoons that can be worked around marsh grass. They can even be caught on spinnerbaits like largemouth bass, and they'll give you a better fight.

23. Saltwater Tips: Using Live Shrimp to Catch Speckled Trout

Live shrimp is a the single most productive saltwater bait for speckled trout when fished at the jetties, off the pier, or around inshore points early in the morning. Biological studies have shown that shrimp make up the bulk of a speckled trout's diet, with the exception of the largest female fish that prefer baitfish for food. Live shrimp will catch those early-rising speckled trout during the spring morning bite. You can catch them in your cast net or buy them at tackle shops and piers, depending on the season.

Keep these tips in mind when fishing live shrimp:

Use a float rig

Since pinfish will likely devour any live shrimp that gets near the bottom use a float rig to keep the shrimp in the feeding column for speckled trout. Float rigs should be adjustable so you can quickly change the depth of the shrimp as the tide comes in and out, and to keep the shrimp away from pinfish and other baitstealers.

Float your live shrimp near the rocks at the jetties or just away from the pier. When inshore float fish near the mouths of the creeks and off points. Let the tide do your work for you, as the natural movement of the water will carry the rig to feeding trout. Specks often stay in slightly deeper water waiting to ambush unwary shrimp that come too close.

Hook the shrimp correctly

The main thing to remember is to never hook a live shrimp in the dark spot near the head, which is a shrimp's brain. Hook them through the 'horns' area. The shrimp should still be active and trying to jump in your hand after hooked.

Alternatively, hook the shrimp through the lower back area for a slightly different effect. Experiment with both ways of hooking the shrimp until you find what is working for trout at the moment.

Pop it just once or twice

If you are using a popping cork don't pop the float rig too often. Once the rig is in the water pop it real hard one time and then let it alone for a minute. This more closely resembles the activity of a live shrimp, and in most cases if a trout is around it will hit as the shrimp is falling back from the first pop.

Jerking the live shrimp around too much won't help, so stick with popping it once and waiting a minute before popping it again. The first pop should be all you need if speckled trout are active in the area.

24. Surf Fishing Tips: What to Use for Bait

Anytime is a great time for surf fishing in the Carolinas. Get out your 10 to 13 foot rods and cast over the whitewater and into the sloughs (pronounced slews) which are the deep holes in the surf where the waves aren't breaking and the fish are gathering. Surf fishing is the ultimate interactive sport as you wade in, knee deep in the foaming saltwater ready to fill up the cooler or fight the big one.

But what do you use for bait?

Here are five of the best baits to use when surf fishing in the Carolinas:

Cut shrimp

Cut shrimp is a great all-around choice for surf fishing, but it should be fresh. Buy shrimp from the seafood market that you would eat yourself. Don't rely on previously frozen 'bait' shrimp sold in tackle shops and at Walmart. Use small pieces of shrimp not huge globs.

Shrimp on number 4 hooks is a fantastic bait for fall spot, croaker, pompano, whiting (sea mullet), black drum, and snapper bluefish. Large, whole dead shrimp can be fished at night in the surf for big sea mullet and redfish.

Sand fleas

They are right there at your feet in the surf, and they are superior surf fishing bait. Those sand fleas (also called mole crabs in some places) that you feel under your feet when walking in the shallow whitewater surf are good for more than just entertaining the kids.

They are the best of all baits for pompano, which are biologically built as sand flea eating machines. Pompano and sand fleas go together. Pompano can even turn themselves sideways in the surf to go shallow and gobble up sand fleas.

Use gold two-hook rigs to fish for pompano in the surf during warm weather and you can fill the cooler. And yes, the female ones that are pregnant with the orange roe in them are the best of all sand fleas to use.

When it comes to gathering sand fleas you can buy specially made rakes, but I have always done it by hand. If you have kids, they are great at this fun activity. Set the little ones to digging you up a bucket full of live sand fleas. Then put them in a bucket with some damp sand and keep it covered and cool. You have your bait right at your feet and the best part is that it's free.

Sand fleas do not just catch pompano. I have also caught sea mullet, flounder, pinfish, croaker, and bluefish on them. Sea mullet (whiting) love them. Hook them up through the shell and fish very shallow in the whitewater surf or just beyond it. You can't miss.

Bloodworms and artificial bloodworms

Bloodworms are the classic go-to bait for spot and will catch just about anything else. They are expensive though, especially in the fall, which is why many folks have switched to the artificial Fishbites bloodworms which work just as well and stay on your hook for fish after fish.

If you are fishing for spot, croaker, snapper bluefish, sea mullet, pompano or any panfish in the surf and want to use bloodworms I'd advise going with the Fishbites artificial 'Bag O' Worms' version. You'll save a ton of money.

Cut mullet and menhaden

Cut mullet is an excellent bait for bluefish and red drum. Most other fish will hit it, though it is not a top spot bait. Big speckled trout will occasionally blast a big chunk of cut mullet and, of course, sharks love it. Most any other fish can be cut up and used for bait. Fresh, bloody cut fish of any kind is usually the best bait for bluefish and sharks in the surf.

Cut mullet or menhaden is also a top choice when surf fishing in areas that have big striped bass runs. Ocean striped bass have their southern terminus near Cape Hatteras, NC and they winter in deep waters off the Outer Banks. In the coldest months surf fishermen gather on these beaches hoping these unpredictable but huge striped bass come near shore.

Live minnows

Although it is a problem keeping live minnows alive while surf fishing they are hands down the best natural surf fishing bait for flounder, and will also catch redfish, speckled trout, bluefish, and Spanish mackerel. You can buy live mud minnows in the store or gather live finger mullet, small pinfish, or pogies (small menhaden) with your cast net.

Fishfinder rigs with egg sinkers and Kahle-style hooks are great for surf fishing live minnows from the beach. Bring the bait back to you in small hops, work it slowly, and the fish will take it from there.

25. Carolina Pier Fishing

The majority of anglers come to Carolina fishing piers to catch bottom fish, which are mainly our many popular and tasty panfish. You can catch spot, croaker, pompano, sea mullet, silver perch, snapper bluefish, red drum, black drum, blowfish and many more species. Flounder anglers will be in the shallow area of the pier fishing live minnows and trying to catch dinner. Out further on the planks Spanish mackerel and bluefish are caught by those throwing plugs, and some piers have great speckled trout runs. At the end of the pier, fishermen use two-rod setups to try and hook up with big brutes like king mackerel, chopper blues, cobia, a wide variety of sharks and even tarpon. Many different varieties of fish can be caught on Carolina fishing piers.

Visiting bottom fishermen should use standard two-hook double drop rigs, which are available in all tackle and pier shops or can be hand-tied. Hooks around size 4 are about right, with some anglers preferring gold hooks for species like pompano. You will want to fish a pyramid or bank sinker at the bottom. Two ounces of weight is usually enough except on days when the current is really strong.

The best bait for bottom fishing is cut fresh shrimp, bloodworms and artificial bloodworms, or live sand fleas where available. Other good baits include fresh cut mullet, squid, and fresh cut bait from any little fish you catch such as pinfish.

Early morning and late afternoon are great times for throwing Gotcha plugs for bluefish and Spanish mackerel, which are both feisty and fun predators that show up as the water warms toward summer. Gotcha plugs (and their many competitors) are pencil plugs with treble hooks that give you amazing casting distance for such a small lure.

These plugs are terrific when worked in the chilly morning or just before a breezy sunset. They should be worked back to the pier in fast bursts and sharp rips. Bluefish favor the redheaded models and Spanish like plugs with gold or silver on them. Speckled and gray trout sometimes like to hit green or blue headed pencil plugs.

Flounder hit in the shallows during most of the pier fishing season, and anglers catch them with live bait around the pilings. People use live mud minnows, finger mullet, or live shrimp to catch flounder on bottom rigs.

Anglers who know what they are doing can catch large sheepshead from our ocean piers on fiddler crabs, clumps of barnacles, or live shrimp. They fish right against the pilings.

Some anglers float fish for speckled trout from the piers using live shrimp. There are also usually a few king mackerel fishermen out at the ends of the fishing piers looking for big game that can include kings, chopper blue-fish, cobia, tarpon, large sting rays, and many different kinds of sharks.

For some reason most people who go up on an ocean fishing pier migrate to the middle of the pier to fish. But usually the best action can be found in the shallow water (which is fine territory for flounder and pompano) just in or outside the whitewater foam of the surf or in the deeper areas where predators like bluefish and Spanish mackerel run.

Fall fishing conditions on the pier can get crowded, and the best way to cast is to swing your rig under the pier and lob it out straight in front of you. This will pay off in less time spent unhooking tangles with other anglers. If you rear back and cast away upwards (and into the wind) you have a lot less control of where your rig is going and the likelihood that you'll become entangled with another angler's rig is far greater.

Most fish are not way out anyway but instead a short distance from the pier. Underhanded lob cast allow you to pinpoint where you put your bait and hit the same spot after you have begun to catch fish.

Although it may be chilly in the morning when you begin pier fishing, fall days can become quite sunny. Make sure you dress in layers so that you can shed clothing as needed and don't let the morning chill or wind fool you-the sun can still give you an angry burn even in the fall. Bring the sunscreen when pier fishing and apply it when you need it.

Fishing from our ocean piers is one of the easiest and most cost effective ways to go saltwater fishing in the Carolinas. Most ocean piers have a blanket license that covers you, so that if you are from out of state you don't have to buy a fishing license. You can have fun for the whole family and have a pretty good chance of catching something to eat for dinner that night.

26. The Best Carolina Seafood Recipes

Sometime if you catch it you want to cook it. Saltwater fish in the Carolinas are among the best fresh seafood. When you keep fish to cook remember to obey state regulations which include size and creel limits on many important species.

The Carolinas also have a long tradition of commercial fishing, and provide a great deal of the fresh seafood for their own citizens and the states beyond. Unfortunately, commercial anglers and recreational anglers have not always had the greatest relationship over the years and fisheries management and politics can get downright ugly.

I'm a recreational angler but I am also a person who loves fresh seafood and buys it readily when I can get it locally. I have always appreciated the commercial fishing industry even if I have not always agreed with the way they are managed by the government.

NC and SC walk a difficult tightrope trying to maintain and oversee our commercial and recreational fisheries. But they are both vital to the tradition and heritage of the

Carolinas, and to our economy. Only by compromise and wise regional management will we find the answers to the user access and fisheries politics questions that have become so divisive.

One thing is for sure: fresh Carolina fish and shellfish are among the best tasting seafood in the world. I have always loved to cook and eat fish and shellfish, and I have collected, cooked, and developed many recipes from friends, books, magazines, websites, and restaurants over the years.

Here is a collection of my favorite Carolina seafood recipes. You can find even more online at my website **Surf and Salt** and my blog **A Dash of Salty**.

Speckled Trout Parmesan

2 lbs speckled trout fillets
1 egg
cup bread crumbs
cup grated Parmesan cheese
small or onion, chopped
olive oil
garlic powder, salt and pepper

Place the onion in a frying pan with enough olive oil to sauté it. Whisk the egg in a bowl. Combine the bread crumbs, cheese, and a dash each of the seasonings.

Coat fish with egg and roll through crumb mixture. Increase the temperature in the frying pan to med high and fry the fish quickly with the sautéd onions, adding a little more olive oil if necessary.

Don't overcook; fish is done when it flakes with a fork. Serve with cocktail sauce on the side. Serves 4.

Beer Battered Spot

8 whole spot, dressed
cup butter, melted
cup beer
2 eggs
1 cup flour
cup cornstarch
veggie oil

Beat the eggs and mix with butter and beer. Stir in flour and cornstarch. Heat oil on high in deep fryer. Dip each spot in batter and then fry until golden brown. Drain on paper towels and serve. Serves 3 to 4.

Carolina Baked Sea Trout

1 whole speckled trout (2-3 lbs), dressed but with the head left on
2 tablespoons lemon juice

2 tablespoons butter (melted)
2 tablespoons white wine
3 tablespoons parsley
3 tablespoons chives

Place sea trout on a large square of aluminum foil. Mix lemon juice, butter, and wine then brush fish with mixture.

Seal and cook at 350 degrees for about 35 minutes. Remove from oven and sprinkle with parsley and chives. Serves 4.

Sautéd Specks in Wine

2 pan-size speckled trout
tablespoon butter
cup mushrooms, diced
1 medium onion, diced
1 cup white wine
salt and pepper to taste

Saute onions and mushrooms until onions are translucent. Add the trout and the white wine; simmer trout until done. Do not overcook. Deglaze pan and pour the mushroom/onion wine sauce over the trout. Serves 2.

Easy Fried Black Drum Chunks

1 lb black drum fillets
House Autry seafood breading
milk
paprika
pepper

salt
veggie oil

Cut black drum fillets into chunks. Rub fillets to taste with paprika, salt and pepper. Dip in milk and then roll in House Autry seafood breading. Fry in hot veggie oil until golden brown. Serves 4.

Spicy Black Drum Nuggets

2 lb black drum fillets, cut into bite-sized chunks
3 eggs, slightly beaten
1/2 cup milk
1/2 cup beer
3 tablespoons prepared mustard
1 teaspoon Tabasco sauce
2 teaspoons salt, divided
2 teaspoons black pepper, divided
1 teaspoon cayenne pepper, divided
3 cups fine yellow corn flour
vegetable oil

In a mixing bowl whisk together eggs, milk, beer, mustard, Tabasco, and half of the salt and pepper. Place black drum in egg mixture, coating well; cover, refrigerate, and let soak for about 1 hour. Mix corn flour with the remaining salt and peppers in a shallow, wide bowl.

Preheat oil in deep fryer to about 370 degrees. Remove black drum from mixture and dredge with corn flour mixture. Fry black drum until the fish nuggets float to the surface and turn golden brown, taking care not to overcook.

Place black drum nuggets on paper towels to drain. Serves
4-6.

Whole Flounder Poached in Clam Broth

1 fresh flounder (3 or 4 lbs), whole dressed with head left on
1 ¼ cups clam juice
1 small onion, diced
½ teaspoon paprika
1 tablespoon butter, melted
dash salt
dash pepper
olive oil

Place whole flounder in a large well-oiled pan (with a lid).
Combine the other ingredients and pour over flounder.
Cover and poach on medium high heat for 15 minutes or
until flounder is done. Do not overcook or fish will be dry.
Serves 3-4.

Sauced Flounder

1 lb flounder fillets
1/3 cup minced onion
1/2 cup fresh mushrooms, chopped
1/2 teaspoon curry powder
1/2 teaspoon paprika
1/2 teaspoon black pepper
1/2 cup white wine
dash salt

Preheat oven to 350 degrees. Arrange flounder fillets in a greased baking dish. Mix wine, onion, mushrooms, and seasonings together and pour over flounder. Bake for 18-20 minutes or until fish is done. Serves 4. Great served with wild rice.

Cheesy Oven-Fried Bluefish

2 lbs bluefish filets
1 cup milk
I cup dry bread crumbs
cup butter or margarine
1/2 teaspoon oregano
1/2 teaspoon garlic powder
tablespoon salt
shredded cheddar cheese

Preheat oven to 500 degrees. Add oregano, garlic powder and salt to crumbs and mix well. Dip fillets in milk and roll in crumb mixture. Place in a well-greased pan, pad butter on top of each fillet. Bake for 10 minutes or until fish flakes easily with a fork. Top fillets with shredded cheese (enough to cover each fillet) 1 minute before the fish is done so it melts over fillets. Serves 4-5.

Oak Island Bluefish Cakes

1 lb bluefish fillets, cooked and diced
2 stalks of celery, diced
½ red pepper, diced
1 small onion, diced
1 small red potatoes, cooked and diced

1 egg, beaten
1 cup bread crumbs
½ teaspoon seafood seasoning
dash Worcestershire sauce
dash hot sauce
olive oil

Mix all ingredients except oil, and blend well. Form into cakes. Heat olive oil on the stove and sauté cakes lightly on both sides. Don't overcook, serve as soon as cakes are golden brown. Serves 4.

Myrtle Beach Basted Pompano

4 pompano, dressed
¼ cup orange juice
2 tablespoons butter
olive oil

Preheat oven to 400 degrees and grease with olive oil. Add pompano and place ½ tablespoon butter over each fish. Pour OJ over fish as well. Bake 12-15 minutes. Serves 2.

Sizzlin Spanish Breakfast

1 lb Spanish mackerel fillets, diced and cooked
4 eggs
½ cup shredded cheddar cheese
1 tablespoon milk
1 tablespoon chili powder

Cook fish first in a little heated olive oil, about 10 minutes sauted in a stove-top pan. Scramble eggs in a frying pan. Add remaining ingredients including cooked fish. Saute about 2 minutes. Serves 2. Serve with toast, OJ and/or Bloody Marys.

Easy Drum and Veggie Soup

This recipe is great with leftover drum if you have some. If you don't have drum you can substitute any firm fish like sheepshead or catfish.

1 lb drum fillets (redfish or black drum), cooked or not
2 cans chicken broth
1 cup sliced mushrooms
1 onion, diced
1 small package frozen mixed vegetables
1 teaspoon Worcestershire sauce
teaspoon garlic salt
teaspoon seafood seasoning OR paprika
dash black pepper
olive oil

Place fillets in a little olive oil and cook until done (if they are not already cooked). Remove fish and chop into chunks. Sauté onion in oil until translucent. Remove onion from oil, discard oil, and combine onion and all other ingredients except fish in pot and bring to boil, then reduce heat.

Add fish and simmer 10 minutes or until veggies are tender. Serve with saltines or oyster crackers. You can top with cheddar cheese if you like. Serves 4 to 5.

Broiled Flounder with Mustard

1 ½ lbs flounder
¼ teaspoon pepper
1 tablespoon olive oil
2 tablespoons prepared brown mustard
2 tablespoons green onions, chopped
1 lime, sliced

Preheat the broiler. Arrange flounder on a baking sheet and sprinkle with pepper then brush with olive oil. Spread prepared brown mustard evenly over the fish. Broil about 3" from the heat source for 2 minutes or until golden brown. Serve with chopped green onions and sliced lime. Serves 4.

Flounder with Shrimp

4 flounder fillets
½ cup flour
2 eggs
1 cup bread crumbs
½ cup butter
½ lb small cooked shrimp
salt
2 tablespoons water
1 lemon, cut into wedges

Sprinkle fillets lightly with salt and roll in flour. In small bowl beat eggs and water. Put bread crumbs on a sheet of wax paper. Dip fish in egg mixture, then coat with bread crumbs. Melt 4 tablespoons butter in frying pan. Sauté fish until browned on both sides, about 4 minutes. Meanwhile melt 2 tablespoons butter in separate frying pan and add shrimp. Toss so that each shrimp is coated with butter. Place shrimp down center of each fillet. Place remaining butter in small saucepan and melt, pour over flounder and serve with lemon wedges. Serves 4.

Baked Flounder and Vegetables in Foil

1 ½ lbs flounder fillets
4 carrots, sliced
8 green onions, sliced
4 zucchini, sliced
1 green bell pepper, sliced
¼ cup teriyaki sauce

Preheat oven to 425° degrees. Divide flounder among sheets of aluminum foil large enough to completely wrap fish and vegetables. Divide carrots, green onions, zucchini and bell pepper and layer on top of fish. Pour teriyaki sauce over vegetables. Bring edges of foil together, fold, and crimp together to close completely. Place foil packets on a baking sheet and bake for 15 minutes or until fish is done. Serves 4.

Broiled Flounder in Lemon Butter

6 small flounder fillets
2 tablespoons butter, melted
½ lemon, juiced
¼ tsp salt
dash pepper
½ lemon, sliced
fresh parsley

Butter a glass baking dish and arrange fillets in the dish. Combine the lemon, butter, salt and pepper and drizzle over the fish; reserve some for use when serving. Broil on highest rack for 8-10 minutes or until fish flakes easily. Garnish with lemon slices and parsley. Serves 4.

Grilled Redfish

1 ½ lbs redfish fillets
3 cloves garlic, peeled and diced
3 shallots, diced
2 jalapeños, diced
1 tablespoon Worcestershire sauce
butter
2 tablespoons fresh cilantro
1 cup fresh sliced tomatoes

Sauté garlic, shallots, and jalapeños in sauce pan with 1 tablespoon butter and Worcestershire sauce. When brown add 1 stick of butter to pan. Melt down and leave on low heat while preparing redfish. Cut slits into skin to keep fillets from curling. Brush butter sauce on fillets until coated and grill over medium high heat. Put fresh cut cilantro and sliced tomatoes on top and baste with butter as needed. When fish flakes take it off grill. Serve over wild rice. Serves 4.

Blackened Redfish

Note: Black drum and sheepshead fillets are also great cooked this way.

8 thick redfish fillets (about ½ inch fillets)
1/2 teaspoons dried thyme leaves
3/4 teaspoons ground black pepper
3/4 teaspoons ground white pepper
1 teaspoon ground cayenne pepper
1 teaspoon garlic powder
1 teaspoon onion powder
2 1/2 teaspoon salt
1 teaspoon paprika
3/4 lb butter, melted
1/2 teaspoons dried oregano leaves

Melt the butter in a small skillet. Heat a large cast-iron skillet over very high heat until it is beyond the smoking stage and you see white ash in the skillet bottom, at least 10 minutes.

Meanwhile pour 2 tablespoons melted butter in 6 small ramekins or other serving bowls; set aside and keep warm. Reserve the remaining butter in its skillet. Thoroughly combine all spices in a small bowl. Dip each fillet in the reserved melted butter so that both sides are well coated; then sprinkle seasoning mix generously and evenly on both sides of the fillets, patting by hand.

Place redfish in the hot skillet and pour 1 teaspoon melted butter on top of each fillet (be careful, as the butter may flame up). Cook, uncovered, over the same high heat until the underside looks charred, about 2 minutes (the time will vary according to the fillet's thickness and the heat of the skillet). Turn the fish over and again pour 1 teaspoon butter on top; cook until fish is done, about 2 minutes more. Repeat with remaining fillets. Serve each fillet while piping hot. To serve, place one fillet and a ramekin of butter on each heated serving plate. Serve with white or wild rice and garlic bread. Serves 4-6.

Quick and Easy Sautéed Redfish

4 medium redfish fillets
2 tablespoons olive oil
flour
salt
pepper
paprika
lemon wedges

Roll fillets in flour and sprinkle with spices to taste. Heat olive oil in a stove top pan and cook fillets uncovered over medium high heat for five minutes. Flip fish and reduce heat to medium, sauté five minutes more or until fish is done. Serve with lemon wedges, great with wild rice. Serves 2.

Flounder Parmesan

2 lbs flounder fillets
1 egg
3/4 cup bread crumbs
1/2 cup grated Parmesan cheese
small or 1/2 onion, chopped
olive oil
garlic powder, salt and pepper

Place the onion in a frying pan with enough olive oil to sauté it. Whisk the egg in a bowl. Combine the bread crumbs, cheese, and a dash each of the seasonings. Coat fish with

egg and roll through crumb mixture. Increase the temperature in the frying pan to med high and fry the fish quickly
with the sautéd onions, adding a little more olive oil if
necessary. Don't overcook; fish is done when it flakes with a
fork. Serve with cocktail sauce on the side. Serves 4.

Beachfront Baked Flounder

2 lbs flounder fillets
1 small onion, chopped
6 tablespoons butter or margarine
2 tablespoons lemon juice
1/8 teaspoon thyme
dash parsley and salt

Preheat oven to 350 degrees. Melt butter and pour into
shallow baking dish. Put fillets in butter, add lemon juice
and thyme, and put onions around the side. Bake 20 minutes,
add a dash of parsley and salt over top with 4 minutes left.
Pour juices over fillets before serving. Serves 4-5.

Oven Baked Flounder

2 lbs thick flounder fillets
1 cup bread crumbs
1 cup milk
1/3 cup butter, melted
1/2 teaspoon garlic powder
1/2 teaspoon oregano
dash salt and pepper

Preheat oven to 500 degrees. Add garlic, oregano, salt and
pepper to bread crumbs. Dip fillets in milk and roll in crumb

mixture. Place on greased baking sheet and drizzle with butter. Bake for 10-12 minutes. Serves 4 to 5.

Southern Fried Flounder

1 1/2 lb flounder fillets
1 cup whole milk
1 cup cornmeal
1 cup pancake mix
veggie oil
lemon wedges
parsley sprigs

In a mixing bowl combine cornmeal and pancake mix and cornmeal, stir. Heat about 2 inches of oil in a heavy skillet (to around 350 degrees).

Place flounder fillets in milk until drenched, then dredge through cornmeal/pancake mix coating well. Deep-fry fillet sin oil, turning once, until golden brown (about 4 1/2 minutes). Dry on paper towels, serve garnished with lemon wedges and parsley springs. Serves 4-5.

Beer Battered Sea Mullet

6 whole sea mullet (whiting), dressed
½ cup butter, melted
½ cup beer
2 eggs
1 cup flour
½ cup cornstarch
vegetable oil

Beat egg yokes and mix with butter and beer. Stir in flour and cornstarch. Beat eggs and add to mixture. Heat oil on med high in fryer or pan. Dip each fish in batter and coat well. Fry until golden brown. Drain on paper towels and serve with hushpuppies and slaw. Serves 2, increase recipe amounts for more fish.

Southport Baked Whiting

4 whole sea mullet (whiting), dressed
¼ lb butter
1 tablespoon lemon juice
1 cup bread crumbs, fine

Preheat oven to 350 degrees. Melt butter and add lemon juice. Dip fish in butter and roll in bread crumbs. Place in a greased baking dish uncovered and bake for 12-15 minutes until done. Serves 2.

Broiled Sea Mullet in Lemon Butter

1 lb sea mullet (whiting) fillets
2 tablespoons butter, melted
1/2 lemon, juiced
1/4 tsp salt
dash pepper
1/2 lemon, sliced
fresh parsley

Butter a glass baking dish and arrange fillets in the dish. Combine the lemon, butter, salt and pepper and drizzle over the fish; reserve some for use when serving. Broil on highest rack for 8-10 minutes or until fish flakes easily. Garnish with lemon slices and parsley. Serves 4.

Carolina Classic Fried Sea Mullet

4 sea mullet, dressed
¾ cup flour
salt and pepper to taste
veggie oil

Cover bottom of frying pan ½ deep with veggie oil and heat on med high until a dash of flour bubbles the oil. Salt and pepper fish. Roll fish in flour until coated well. Place fish in pan and cook until golden brown. Do not overcook. Serve with hushpuppies, French fries, slaw, and sweat tea.

Beaufort Crab Cakes

1 lb crab meat
2 tablespoons flour
2 tablespoons butter, melted
2 tablespoons mayonnaise
Juice of ½ lemon
1 teaspoon mustard
½ teaspoon crab boil seasoning
1 egg, beaten
Salt and pepper to taste
Cracker meal

Combine all ingredients except egg and salt and pepper. Beat egg with salt and pepper added. Form crab mixture into cakes. Roll each cake in cracker meal, dip in egg, then roll again in cracker meal. Fry in hot oil until brown. Serves 6.

Sunset Crab Cakes

1 lb crab meat
¾ cup saltine crackers
1 large egg
2 tablespoons minced onions
2 tablespoons mayonnaise
1 teaspoon Worcestershire sauce
1 teaspoon Dijon mustard
1 teaspoon Tabasco sauce
1 teaspoon salt

Mix ingredients together, reserving some cracker crumbs. Form 3-inch patties. Roll in remaining crumbs. Fry in oil until brown. Serves 6.

Carolina Crab Cakes

1 lb crab meat
1 egg, beaten
1 green pepper, chopped
1 tablespoon chopped dried onion
1 teaspoon dried mustard
1/3 cup bread crumbs
3 tablespoons mayonnaise
dash salt and pepper

Place all ingredients in a bowl and mix together, forming into cakes. Cook cakes in hot vegetable oil, at least three minutes on each side. Serves 5.

Bluefish with Almond Crust

8 bluefish fillets, about 6 ounces each
2 eggs
1 cup freshly grated Parmesan cheese
1 teaspoon lemon pepper
1 teaspoon garlic pepper
1 cup ground almonds
1/4 cup all-purpose flour
6 tablespoons butter
8 sprigs parsley
8 lemon wedges

Mix the eggs with the lemon pepper and garlic pepper and beat until blended and set aside. Stir together ground almonds with Parmesan cheese in a shallow dish until combined and set aside. Dust the bluefish with flour. Dip the bluefish in egg mixture, then press into the almond mixture.

Melt butter in a large skillet over medium-high heat. Cook bluefish in melted butter until golden brown on both sides. Reduce heat to medium-low. Sprinkle the bluefish with the remaining Parmesan cheese, cover, and continue cooking until the Parmesan cheese has melted. Garnish with parsley springs and lemon wedges to serve. Serves 4.

Grilled Snapper Bluefish

Snapper bluefish are small bluefish, and the tastiest are those that weigh a pound or less each. Check size limits in the state you are fishing in before you keep a snapper bluefish.

8 snapper bluefish, dressed
olive oil
salt
pepper
lemon juice

Rub bluefish all over with oil and sprinkle with lemon juice. Sprinkle with salt and pepper.

Grill over medium high heat about 6-7 minutes for each side. Great with wild rice. Serves 4.

Grilled Bluefish with Black Olives

This recipe is for thick fillets from chopper bluefish, which are larger bluefish over 5 lbs.

2 lbs thick bluefish fillets
Italian salad dressing
1 ½ cup black olives, drained, pitted and chopped
½ cup olive oil
½ teaspoon black pepper
½ teaspoon Cayenne pepper
½ cup chopped Italian parsley
Mix all ingredients but bluefish and salad dressing in a bowl and set aside. Marinate bluefish in Italian dressing for at least three hours in the fridge.

On a well-oiled grill cook bluefish fillets 10 minutes per inch of thickness. Place cooked fish in a microwave-safe pan and spread black olive mixture over bluefish. Microwave for 1 minute, remove bluefish to platter and serve. Serves 5-6.

Bluefish Parmesan

2 lbs bluefish fillets
1 egg
1 cup bread crumbs
½ cup grated Parmesan cheese
small onion, chopped
garlic powder, couple dashes
salt and pepper, couple dashes each
olive oil

Place the onion in a frying pan with enough olive oil to sauté
it.

Meanwhile, whisk the egg in a bowl. Combine the bread
crumbs, cheese, and a dash each of the seasonings. Coat
bluefish with egg and roll through crumb mixture.

Increase the temperature in the frying pan to med high and
fry the bluefish quickly with the sautéed onions, adding a
little more olive oil if necessary. Don't overcook; bluefish is
done when it flakes with a fork. Serve with cocktail sauce on
the side. Serves 4.

Flounder Au Gratin

1 ½ lbs flounder fillets
2 tablespoons chopped onion
2 tablespoons chopped celery
2 tablespoons lemon juice
2 tablespoons butter
1 cup milk
flour, to taste

salt and pepper, to taste
½ cup grated cheddar cheese

Preheat oven to 450 degrees. Put the fillets in a shallow
baking pan. Sprinkle with onions, celery, salt and pepper.
Add lemon juice and 2 tablespoons water to pan. Bake for
10 minutes.

In separate pan melt butter and stir in flour. Gradually stir in
milk and cook until it thickens. Reserving 2 tablespoons for
garnish, add cheese and heat until melted. Pour over fish
then sprinkle remaining cheese on top. Bake for 12 minutes
more.

Cajun Scallops

1 lb bay scallops
1 teaspoon olive oil
1 large red onion, separated into rings
1 teaspoon Cajun seasoning
½ teaspoon black pepper
1 teaspoon butter
1 garlic clove
2 teaspoons hot sauce

Heat oil in a cast iron skillet over high heat. Add onion,
Cajun seasoning, and pepper and sauté 3 minutes.

Add butter and garlic, sauté 30 seconds.

Add scallops, cook 1 minute. Sprinkle with hot sauce, turn.
Cook 3 minutes more. Serves 2.

Coconut Breaded Scallops

32 sea scallops
3 cups wheat beer
3 cups all-purpose flour
2 teaspoons baking powder
1 egg
2 teaspoons garlic salt
1 teaspoon salt
1 teaspoon white pepper
2 cups shredded coconut
2 cups panko

Lightly marinate scallops in iced water with salt and white pepper for 15 minutes. Mix shredded coconut and panko, set aside. Blend remaining ingredients to make a fresh beer batter. Dip scallops in beer batter then roll in coconut mix. Deep fry until golden brown. Serves 4.

Easy Pan Fried Scallops

2 lbs fresh sea scallops
flour
6 tablespoons butter
garlic salt
chopped parsley

Lightly coat the scallops with flour. Heat butter in stove top pan. Sauté scallops in butter 4 minutes on each side. Sprinkle to taste with garlic salt while cooking. Serve garnished with parsley. Serves 4 to 6.

Scallop and Shrimp Kabobs

½ lb sea scallops
½ lb shrimp, peeled and deveined
1 green pepper cut into chunks
1 red pepper cut into chunks
1 can pineapple chunks, drain but reserve juice
½ lb fresh mushrooms
1 onion, cut into pieces

*marinade: pineapple juice from can, ¼ cup wine vinegar,
1/3 cup olive oil, 1 teaspoon salt, ½ teaspoon pepper, 1
teaspoon minced fresh ginger*

Thread all items and marinade overnight in the fridge. Grill
over hot coals until shrimp curl and turn pink. Can be served
with melted butter. Serves 4.

Black Drum Parmesan

1 lb black drum fillets
1 lemon
1/3 cup Parmesan cheese
1/2 cup white wine
3 pats butter
1/3 cup bread crumbs

Place black drum in broiling pan. Add wine. Sprinkle bread
crumbs and Parmesan cheese over fish and top with pats of
margarine if desired. Broil for 10-15 minutes until fish turns
opaque. Serve with lemon slices. Serves 2.

Oven Fried Black Drum

2 lbs black drum fillets
1 cup milk
I cup dry bread crumbs
1/4 cup butter or margarine
1/2 teaspoon oregano
1/2 teaspoon garlic powder
1/2 tablespoon salt
shredded cheddar cheese

Preheat oven to 500 degrees. Add oregano, garlic powder
and salt to crumbs and mix well. Dip black drum fillets in
milk and roll in crumb mixture. Place in a well-greased pan,
pad butter on top of each fillet. Bake for 10 minutes or until
fish flakes easily with a fork. Top black drum fillets with
shredded cheese (enough to cover each fillet) 1 minute
before the fish is done so it melts over fillets. Serves 4-5.

Creole Black Drum

2 lbs black drum fillets
3 tomatoes, chopped
1 small onion, chopped
1/2 green pepper, chopped
1 tablespoon lemon juice
Cayenne pepper to taste
3 tablespoons butter
olive oil

Preheat oven to 400 degrees. Melt the butter in a small sauce
pan. Coat a large baking dish with olive oil and lay black
drum fillets inside it. Top black drum with remaining ingre-

dients and pour butter over dish. Bake 15-20 minutes until fish is done. Great with wild rice. Serves 4-5.

Marinated Shark Steaks

2 lbs shark steaks
½ cup white wine
¼ cup salad oil
1 teaspoon Dijon mustard
1 teaspoon salt
½ teaspoon pepper
1 clove garlic, minced

Place shark in a flat dish. Combine remaining ingredients and pour over shark. Marinate at least one hour in the refrigerator. Remove fish from marinade and grill, 4 minutes per side, until shark flakes easily. Serves 6.

Deep Fried Shark

2 lbs shark fillets
1 cup flour
1 teaspoon salt
½ teaspoon white pepper
1 teaspoon baking powder
1 cup water
1 tablespoon vinegar
Oil

Cut shark into 1-inch cubes. Mix flour, salt, pepper, and baking powder and slowly add water and vinegar. Let stand 15 minutes. Heat oil 425 degrees. Dip pieces of fish into batter and fry several pieces at a time until brown.

Barbecued Shark Steaks

4 thick shark steaks
2 large onions, chopped
2 cups hickory-smoked barbecue sauce
1/2 cup pineapple juice
1/2 cup orange juice
1 cup cider vinegar
2 tablespoons olive oil

Chop onions very fine and sauté them in a little olive oil on stove top until they are cooked and translucent. Let cool then put onions (with oil) in a large bowl and combine with all other ingredients to make a marinade (mix well). Pour marinade over shark steaks and refrigerate. Marinate shark at least 3 hours. Grill over medium high heat until fish is done. Serves 2.

Barbecued Fish Tacos

4 (8-inch) tortillas
1 lb flounder, trout, amberjack or other lean mild fish fillet
¼ teaspoon salt
¼ teaspoon pepper
¼ cup barbecue sauce
Veggie cooking spray
Sour cream
Sliced green onions
Lime wedges

Wrap tortillas in aluminum foil. Bake at 350 for 10 minutes. Sprinkle fish with salt and pepper, lightly brush each side with barbeque sauce. Place fish in grilled basket coved with cooking spray. Cook, covered with grill id, over medium coals 5 minutes on each side. Remove fish from basket and flake gently with a fork.

Spoon fish evenly down the center of the tortillas, top with sour crème and green onions. Squeeze lime wedges over tortillas; fold opposite sides over filling. Serves 4.

Guilty King Mackerel

1 stick butter
3 lbs king mackerel steaks/fillets
½ onion, diced
1 green pepper, diced
Shredded cheddar cheese
Oyster crackers

Place butter in saucepan. Melt over med heat. When melted add mackerel, onion and green pepper. Turn heat very low; cover. Cook 1 hour until fish is white and flaky. Stir occasionally, breaking up fish. Serve in a bowl with a sprinkling of shredded cheddar cheese on top and oyster crackers. Serves 6.

Flounder Potato Bake

1 ½ lb potatoes, peeled, thinly sliced
6 tablespoons olive oil
1 tablespoon minced garlic
1/3 cup chopped parsley
Onion salt
Pepper
1 ½ lbs flounder fillets

Place potatoes in cold water, drain, and pat dry. Combine oil, garlic and parsley in a cup.

In a 9 x 10 inch baking dish mix potatoes with half seasoned oil. Sprinkle with onion salt and pepper. Bake at 450 degrees for 15 minutes or until potatoes are nearly tender. Remove from oven and place flounder on potatoes. Drizzle with remaining oil. Sprinkle with onion salt and pepper. Bake 12-15 minutes, basting occasionally with pan juices. Serves 4-5.

Sweet Vidalia Onion Fish Steaks

4 large fish steaks, king mackerel, tuna, mahi-mahi or shark
2 large Vidalia onions, chopped
2 cups hickory-smoked barbecue sauce
½ cup pineapple juice
½ cup orange juice
1 cup cider vinegar
olive oil

Chop onions **very** fine, and sauté them in a little olive oil until they are cooked and translucent. Put onions in a large bowl and combine with all other ingredients. Stir well and refrigerate. Marinate fish steaks in Sweet Vidalia Onion Marinade for at least 3 hours. Grill over hot coals, brushing with marinade, for 13-16 minutes. Serves 4.

Grilled Tuna Teriyaki

bluefin (or other) tuna steaks
teriyaki sauce
soy sauce
olive oil

honey
onion
fresh garlic
fresh ginger

Amount of marinade is dependent on how many tuna steaks you have. Use 1 part teriyaki sauce, ¾ part soy sauce, ¼ part olive oil, and ¼ part honey. Add diced onion, fresh garlic and fresh ginger to taste. Grill steaks over hot coals about six minutes, flipping once.

Pirate's Bloody Fish Steaks

4 fish steaks, king mackerel, swordfish, shark, mahi-mahi, or tuna
½ cup rum
½ cup Kikkoman soy sauce
½ cup A-1 steak sauce
1 cup tomato sauce
5 tablespoons Worcestershire sauce
3 tablespoons hot sauce (optional)

Combine all ingredients except fish in a bowl and stir well. Marinate fish steaks in Pirate's Bloody Marinade for at least 2 hours. Grill over hot coals for 15 minutes, brushing with marinade. Serves 4.

Honey Fried Striped Bass

1 lb striped bass fillets
2 tablespoons honey
4 tablespoons butter

1 lemon
½ cup cornmeal
¼ cup flour
½ teaspoon salt
½ teaspoon pepper
1 egg
1/3 cup milk

Mix cornmeal, flour, salt and pepper in bowl. Mix egg and milk in separate bowl. Rub striped bass with lemon and dredge in cornmeal mixture. Dip striped bass in milk mixture and then back into cornmeal mixture. Heat butter to almost smoking in frying pan. Put striped bass in pan and cook until golden brown on both sides. Put honey on top of striped bass then lower heat, cover, and cook for a few minutes. Serves 4.

Jeffrey's Striped Bass for Daughters

6 striped bass fillets
1 cup flour
1 cup cornmeal
dash each black pepper, Cayenne pepper, garlic powder, and salt
milk
olive oil

Heat olive oil in skillet on medium heat. Combine flour, cornmeal, and spices in a shallow dish and mix. Dip fillets in milk and then dredge through flour mixture coating fish thoroughly and evenly. Fry fillets in hot olive oil for 4 minutes, turn and fry 3 minutes or until fish is done.

Drain on paper towels and serve with cream soda and Organic Macaroni & Cheese. Serves 3.

Breakfast Striped Bass

1 striped bass fillet
1 Vidalia onion, sliced
orange juice
2 oranges
1 lemon

Marinate the fillet in orange juice for six hours. Discard the orange juice marinate.
Place aluminum foil inside a baking pan. Put the striped bass fillet in the middle. Pour new orange juice until it covers the fish half way. Cover the top of the fillet with sliced Vidalia onions and sliced orange and lemon. Cover the orange slices with sliced lemon. Seal the aluminum foil to retain the juices while baking. Bake at 400 degrees until fish flakes easily.

When done, remove the cooked orange slices and lemon slices. Before serving, squeeze fresh orange juice over the fillet. Serve with the onion slices on top and garnish with orange slices. Serves 1.

Creamy Striped Bass

2 lb striped bass fillets
2 tablespoons butter
1 cup sour cream
1/3 cup grated Parmesan cheese
1 cup onions, sliced
1 tablespoon lemon juice

1 teaspoon garlic powder
1 teaspoon oregano
1/4 cup olive oil

Arrange fillets in a buttered baking dish. Combine sour
cream, grated cheese, lemon juice and spread over fish. Top
with onion slices. Bake into a 350°F degree oven for 15
minutes or until fish is tender. Serves 4-5.

Broccoli-Stuffed Flounder

8 flounder fillets
2 tablespoons butter, melted
1 tablespoon lemon juice
1 teaspoon salt
1/4 teaspoon pepper
1 (10 ounce) package frozen chopped broccoli, thawed and
drained
1 cup cooked rice
1 cup shredded cheddar cheese
paprika

In a small bowl combine the butter, lemon juice, salt and
pepper. In another bowl combine the broccoli, rice, cheese
and half of the butter mixture. Spoon 1/2 cup onto each
flounder fillet. Roll up and place seam side down in a baking
dish coated with nonstick cooking spray. Pour remaining
butter mixture over roll-ups. Bake, uncovered, at 350 degrees for 20-24 minutes or until fish flakes easily with a
fork. Baste with pan drippings, sprinkle with paprika. Serves
4.

Blue Crab Bacon Rolls

1 cup blue crab meat
½ cup tomato juice
1 egg, beaten
1 cup dry bread crumbs
1 tablespoon parsley
1 teaspoon paprika
1 teaspoon black pepper
12 slices bacon, cut in half

Mix tomato juice and egg, add remaining ingredients except bacon. Mix thoroughly and shape into 24 finger-length rolls. Wrap each roll with bacon and fasten with a toothpick. Broil, turning frequently, until brown.

Delicious Clams in the Shell

You can use this recipe as an appetizer or part of a seafood meal.

24 small clams in shell
4 slices bacon, cooked until crisp and crumbled
1/4 cup butter, softened
1/4 cup finely chopped celery
1/4 cup chopped green onion
1/4 cup finely chopped green bell pepper
1 tablespoon lemon juice
salt

Open clams and remove clams from shell. Wash shells, place each clam in deep half of shell. Discard remaining clam shell halves.

Sprinkle clams with a little salt. Blend butter, chopped green onion, chopped bell pepper, chopped celery, lemon juice, and crumbled bacon. Top each clam with a tablespoon of the butter and vegetable mixture.

Arrange the clams on a shallow baking pan. Bake at 425 degrees for 12 minutes. Serves 4.

Sautéd Shrimp and Mushrooms

1 ½ lbs medium shrimp, shelled and deveined
3 tablespoons soy sauce
2 tablespoons sherry
3 stalks of celery and leaves
3 scallions
½ lb mushrooms
3 tablespoons olive oil
½ teaspoon seafood seasoning

Combine soy sauce, sherry, and seasonings. Pour over shrimp and mix, let sit 15 minutes in refrigerator. Slice celery, scallions and mushrooms. Heat frying pan with olive oil on med high, add celery and scallions and sauté for 4 minutes. Add mushrooms and shrimp, sauté until shrimp turns pink 3-5 minutes. Serves 4-5. Great with wild rice or rice pilaf.

Fish and Shellfish Au Gratin

1/2 pound fish fillets
1 onion, chopped
1 pound fresh shrimp, peeled and deveined
1/2 pound small scallops

1 pound fresh crabmeat
1 green bell pepper, chopped
1 cup butter, divided
1 cup all-purpose flour, divided
4 cups water
3 cups milk
1 cup shredded sharp Cheddar cheese
1 tablespoon distilled white vinegar
1 teaspoon Worcestershire sauce
1/2 teaspoon salt
1/2 teaspoon black pepper
1 dash hot pepper sauce
1/2 cup grated Parmesan cheese

In a heavy skillet sauté the onion and the pepper in 1/2 cup of butter. Cook until tender. Mix in 1/2 cup of the flour and cook over medium heat for 10 minutes, stirring frequently. Stir in crabmeat, remove from heat, and set aside.

In a large Dutch oven, bring the water to a boil. Add the shrimp, scallops, and fish and simmer for 3 minutes. Drain, reserving 1 cup of the cooking liquid, and set the seafood aside.

In a heavy saucepan melt the remaining 1/2 cup butter over low heat. Stir in remaining 1/2 cup flour. Cook and stir constantly for 1 minute. Gradually add the milk plus the 1 cup reserved cooking liquid. Raise heat to medium. Cook, stirring constantly, until the mixture is thickened and bubbly. Mix in the shredded Cheddar cheese, vinegar, Worcestershire sauce, salt, pepper, and hot sauce. Stir in cooked seafood.

Preheat oven to 350 degrees . Lightly grease baking dish. Press crabmeat mixture into the bottom. Spoon the seafood mixture over the crabmeat crust, and sprinkle with the Parmesan cheese. Bake in the preheated oven for 30 minutes, or until lightly browned. Serves 8.

Baked Seafood Lasagna

1/2 pound scallops
1/2 pound fish fillets
1/2 shrimp, peeled and deveined
1 onion, chopped
2 tablespoons butter
12 ounces cottage cheese
1 (8 ounce) package cream cheese
2 teaspoons dried basil
1/2 teaspoon salt
1/8 teaspoon ground black pepper
1 egg
2 (10.75 ounce) cans condensed cream of mushroom soup
1/3 cup milk
1 clove garlic, minced
1/2 cup white wine
1 (16 ounce) package lasagna noodles
2 ounces shredded mozzarella cheese
2 tablespoons grated Parmesan cheese

Cook the lasagna noodles in a large pot of boiling salted water until al dente. Drain. Sauté onion in the butter. Combine the cottage cheese, cream cheese, basil, salt, pepper, egg, and sautéed onion. Set aside. Combine the mushroom soup, milk, and garlic. Stir in the white wine , bay scallops, flounder fillets, and shrimp. Set aside.

Assemble ingredients in a greased lasagna pan as follows: a thin layer of seafood sauce, 1/5 noodles, 1/2 cheese mixture, 1/5 noodles, 1/2 seafood mixture, 1/5 noodles, 1/2 cheese mixture, 1/5 noodles, 1/2 seafood mixture, and remaining noodles. Place mozzarella cheese and Parmesan cheese on the top.

Bake at 350 for 50 minutes. Remove from oven. Serves 6.

Festival Speckled Trout

This is a great speckled trout recipe for cooking big speck-led trout whole, which is the best way not to waste any trout meat.

2 whole speckled trout about 2 ½ to 3 lbs each, cleaned and dressed
Lemon and lime wedges
2 cloves garlic minced
2 tablespoons olive oil
2 onions, finely chopped
1 cup green pepper, seeded and chopped
1 cup red pepper, seeded and chopped
8 ounces shredded cheddar cheese
12 tomatillos, thinly sliced then chopped
1 cup dry white wine
Butter spray for baking dish

Score flesh on sides of speckled trout ¼ inch deep every 1 ½ inches. Insert lemon wedges, peel side out.

Cook garlic in olive oil in skillet over med high heat. Add onions and cook until translucent. Add peppers, cook 2 more minutes. Place in large bowl and stir in cheese and tomatillos.

Stuff speckled trout cavity with the cheese mixture. Tie fish closed.

Preheat oven to 375 degrees. Place speckled trout in baking dish greased with butter spray. Pour wine over fish and bake fish 30 minutes. Remove string and transfer to serving platter. Garnish with lemon and line wedges. Makes 4-6 servings.

Beer Battered Pan Trout

8 whole pan-sized speckled trout, dressed
1/2 cup butter, melted
1/2 cup beer
2 eggs
1 cup flour
1/2 cup cornstarch
veggie oil

Beat eggs and mix with butter and beer. Stir in flour and cornstarch. Heat oil on high in deep fryer. Dip each speckled trout in batter and then fry until golden brown. Drain on paper towels and serve. Serves 3 to 4.

Manhattan-Style Fish Chowder

You can use any hearty, white fish for this recipe...such as bass, drum, catfish or sheepshead.

1 lb fish fillets, cut into 1-inch pieces
1 can minced clams
8 slices bacon
1/2 cup onion, chopped
1/4 cup green pepper, chopped
1/2 cup celery, chopped
1/2 head cabbage, chopped
1 cup potatoes, diced
1 cup chicken broth
2 cups tomato juice
1/4 teaspoon Cayenne pepper
1 teaspoon seafood seasoning
three dashes Worcestershire sauce

Fry bacon until lightly browned, crumble and return to grease. Add onion, green pepper, and celery; cook until tender. Add broth, cabbage, potatoes, and seafood seasoning. Bring to a boil and reduce heat, simmer 10 minutes.

Add fish and clams along with tomato juice, Cayenne pepper and Worcestershire sauce, return to just under boil and cook until potatoes are done, about 5 more minutes. Serves 6 to 7, serve with saltine crackers.

Easy Seafood Chowder

2 slices bacon
1 lb shrimp, peeled and deveined
1 small can minced clams
1 medium onion, chopped
1 can cream of potato soup
1 teaspoon black pepper
milk

Fry bacon and onion until onion is tender. Crumble bacon. Prepare soup with milk according to can. Mix all ingredients in soup pot and simmer 15 minutes. Serve with oyster crackers. Serves 4 to 5.

Grilled Pompano

4 pompano, dressed
2 tablespoons soy sauce
2 tablespoons orange juice
2 tablespoons lemon juice
2 tablespoons tomato juice
tablespoon garlic salt
fresh black pepper to taste

Mix all ingredients except fish. Marinate pompano in other ingredients for no more than 20 minutes. Grill on medium high heat on grill about 6 minutes on each side. You can melt some butter and pour over the fish at the end if you want, though be aware of the calorie and fat increase if you do. Serves 2.

Greek-Style Clam Chowder

Buy inexpensive New England Clam Chowder at the store (not condensed, a brand like Progresso or something similar) and add your own ingredients to make it Greek. Your guest will think you're a gourmet chef!

2 cans New England Clam Chowder
1 tablespoon oil
½ cup red bell pepper, chopped
1 cup mushrooms, sliced

½ cup chopped onion
1 can artichoke hearts, drained
½ cup water
½ teaspoon seafood seasoning
½ teaspoon black pepper

Cook onion and bell pepper in oil for a few minutes until tender. Add all remaining ingredients and stir gently to blend.

Simmer covered over medium heat 30 minutes, stirring occasionally (don't boil). Serve with oyster crackers. Great topped with shredded cheddar cheese.

Makes about 6 servings.

27. Carolina Kayak Fishing

Kayak fishing is becoming a very popular way for Carolina anglers to go fishing these days, as it combines a wonderfully interactive nature experience with a fun fishing trip. You can fish from a kayak on many freshwater lakes, rivers, and ponds and even get in on some fun kayak fishing in saltwater estuaries and waterways.

Make sure you take basic kayaking lessons or learn from an experienced kayaker before you get out on the water. Knowing the basics helps you avoid discomfort or injury due to improper paddling or mishandled equipment. Kayaking can be a very relaxing sport, but it can also be very strenuous.

Try out a friend's kayak or a rental before you buy to be sure you know what you want. Purchase a brightly colored kayak for safety and stay away from blue or gray colors that will blend in with the water. Safety is more important than style.

Make sure you wear a personal floatation device (PFD) while paddling. Remember that a kayak floats but an angler doesn't. Also take along plenty of liquids so you don't get dehydrated while doing all that paddling.

Buy a sturdy paddle. Top models are usually lighter than heavy, cheaper models and will really make a difference when you are paddling. Taking along a bilge pump and an extra paddle is not a bad idea.

Pay close attention to the weather if you are going kayak fishing and make sure you plan for the current if you are on a river or in a saltwater estuary. River currents and coastal tides vary in intensity so make sure you are aware of what you are getting into.

A six to seven foot rod is a good average choice for kayak fishing. Lighter gear can be used in still water while those out in saltwater will want longer and sturdier rods. You can get away with a bit lighter gear than you think because your kayak actually acts as part of your drag.

Today's soft tackle boxes are a great boon to kayak fishing. Find one you like with at least three removable plastic trays for your lures.

Kayak fishing is fun and great exercise. Don't forget a safety leash between your rod and the kayak so you don't lose your fishing gear. And always keep safety in mind first when kayak fishing.

28. Summertime Carolina Shark Fishing

Some folks think of shark fishing in terms of huge rods, big bloody baits and the movie Jaws. But the truth is you can have a lot of summertime fun in the Carolina salt-water surf catching small sharks. Small dogfish sharks as well as other shark species provide a lot of feisty fighting action when the usual inshore surf and pier fish are nowhere to be found.

The dogs days of summer in the south are a time for hitting the beach, but surf fishermen often find themselves out of luck as redfish, speckled trout, Spanish mackerel, pompano, flounder and bluefish will often stage bites in the early hours of summertime mornings and then stop biting once the sun is high in the sky not to be seen again all day.

Thankfully pier and surf anglers can still have some fun fishing for small sharks. Dogfish sharks invade the southern saltwater surf in the hottest temperatures and are always available to bite. They are in the shallows feeding on small minnows, crabs, and sand fiddlers. Very few folks eat dogfish sharks but they are still awful fun to catch and the kids love to see and touch them. If you catch one and don't intend to keep it you should never kill it but instead return it to the water as these small sharks are an important part of the food chain in the surf.

Dogfish sharks will bite just about any natural bait, and can easily be caught on cut shrimp, sand fiddlers, squid or any cut fish. If they are in the surf they will be just about impossible to keep off your bottom rig. They rarely hit artificial lures as they rely almost entirely on their sense of smell to hit baits and have a very limited eyesight. On occasion, though, they will even smack a slowly fished synthetic grub or a spoon you put right in front of them.

Mixed in with the dogfish during the summer will be larger sharks. Hammerheads, bonnetheads, sharpnose, sandsharks, and tiger sharks are among the species that swim among the Atlantic surf and can occasionally be caught by fishermen. These brutes will give you a real fight on light tackle.

Sharks are a highly regulated species so make sure you check the regulations for the state that you are fishing before you keep one. Some shark species are prohibited from the take, and some have strict size and creel limits.

Shark fishing can be a lot of fun, and it provides something to do during the summer when gamefish just won't come out and cooperate in the heat. Sharks put up a good fight and most can be shown to the kids and quickly returned to the water unharmed. Shark fishing is a fast-action and occasionally thrilling light tackle and surf fishing sport.

By the way, sharks are also one of the few species present around piers and in the surf in the dead of winter. Some ocean piers even have winter dogfish tournaments. They provide great sport and a lot of fun when nothing else is biting.

29. Backwater and Inlet Shore Fishing Tips

If you are in the gas saving mood or don't own a boat, shore fishing is a quick and easy fishing option. Access to the our saltwater creeks, waterways, rivers and beaches is not what it once was, but there are still places out there to fish and have a lot of inexpensive fun.

Shore fishing can be productive in many saltwater areas. The number one key is not to overlook the obvious: fish tend to gravitate to structure and that's where you should start. Hard structure like piers, bridges, rock piles and docks are almost always holding some fish.

Anything with pilings in the water holds opportunities. Many different fish like hanging around places with such pilings, since that's where the smaller critters they eat hang around. Some fish, like sheepshead or flounder, may be right up against or within feet of the pilings, whereas roamers like redfish and speckled trout swim around hard structure often switching feeding areas as the wind or current changes and bait drifts in different directions.

Many fish can often be found beside the pilings or a little bit downstream. Weeds or marsh grass around shore are also great areas to fish as species like trout and redfish will seek both food and cover from predatory birds.

Live bait is a good option for shore fishing. If you buy and learn to throw a cast net it will pay you back many times over. The best bait is usually the small critters you can catch in your cast net that the local fish are feeding on.

Cut bait is also a good option. Cut shrimp, bloodworms, earthworms, Fishbites bloodworms or cut bait from any fresh caught fish will work. So will clam meat and those scurrying fiddler crabs.

Lures work as well. You want heavier lures you can throw some distance from shore, since you can't cover quite as much ground as you can in a boat. MirrOlures and other plugs are good, but don't throw them near structure you haven't fished before if you don't want to lose them. Today's scented soft baits on lead head jigs are great for easy fishing and covering a lot of ground, and they really do work.

When shore fishing you need to get decent casting distance, but don't use more weight than you need to get your bait or lure to the bottom. Simple rigs with split shots or small egg sinkers are what you want if the current is not too rough where you are fishing.

There are a lot of old bridges and lonely looking docks in the Carolina rivers and waterways that hold fish. If you can find access you might be surprised at what you can catch.

Fish slowly around the pilings and use live bait on fishfinder rigs or those scented baits. I've been on a lot of fishing expeditions where an old bridge, pier, or dock turned out to be harboring nice-sized flounder, speckled trout, redfish or black drum.

No matter what fuel costs people will still be out there fishing in boats because it is so much fun. But shore fishing is a viable inexpensive option and can be just as fun. Some of my best fishing experiences have come while taking fish after fish from shore, while the guys in the boats looked on with envy.

30. Catching Fall Spot on Fishbites Artificial Bloodworms

     Spot are a relatively small saltwater panfish that are a big deal to Carolina fishermen in the fall. Traditionally, the autumn spot run is a time for anglers to pack pier pilings and inlet mouths catching the little fish, which are cousins of the larger and more glamorous redfish and speckled trout and just right for the frying pan. A mess of fall spot is the most popular seafood dish in the fall in the Carolinas.

     Spot are caught on bottom rigs, usually two-hook rigs, held down by 2 or 3 ounce sinkers. They run in the surf and in the inshore waterways and rivers. In the fall folks fish the left side of the piers which faces north or east, because spot are running down the coast and will not go under a pier. You will often see fall piers packed with people only fishing the left side.

     Traditionally the best bait for spot is live bloodworms, cut up into small pieces. Live bloodworms are imported into the Carolinas from Maine and Canada and are a very expensive bait, however, and for years tackle shops and bait stores would jack up the prices in the fall (frankly, they still do) so that a bag of bloodworms can run anywhere from $8 to $13 and even higher ridiculous numbers.

Fortunately in the last few years science has given Carolina spot anglers a break. The company Fishbites out of Florida, which makes artificial synthetic cut baits, came out with an artificial bloodworm cut bait that is sold as 'Bag O' Worms.'

Fishermen soon found out that the artificial bloodworms work every bit as good as the real thing, and in fact better since the mesh in them helps them to stay on the hook so that you can catch spot after spot on the same little piece. This is a huge money-saver for spot fishermen over buying live bloodworms.

If you want to purchase some Fishbites artificial bloodworms you can get them at any of the local coastal tackle shops, or even order them online through my website **Surf and Salt**.

I promise you won't be disappointed in the Fishbites bloodworms. They are a definite boon to those of us who love to fish the Carolina piers and inlets for spot in the fall but don't want to pay those high bloodworm prices.

31. Two Funny Carolina Fishing Stories

I can't write this book without telling my two funniest fishing stories. They won't help you catch any fish but they may give you a chuckle.

The Bait in the Trailer Story

For as long as I can remember, my family has had a place at Ocean Isle Beach. I grew up in Fayetteville, NC two hours inland, but when we went on vacation we always went to Ocean Isle. A house is now on the property, but at the time of this story (back in the late 1980s) there was just a trailer there.

I was in college and sometimes my dad would let me use the trailer on fishing trips, which usually meant a little fishing and a lot of beer drinking. One time I went down with my high school buddies John Teeters and Lane Benton. We drank a lot of beer (I drank the most) and fished a little bit.

Now, you have to know about my dad. He is sorta the opposite of me and likes everything kept neat and orderly. He was always getting on me about making sure the trailer was clean when I was leaving it, which I apparently (under the influence) kept reminding John and Lane about time and time again on this trip.

Well, at the end of the trip it was time to go. The place was a wreck after a few days of just us young bucks staying there, but I had a huge hangover and wanted to leave. So instead of helping John and Lane clean up I just put a few things in order and left in my car, leaving them the keys and telling them to do the cleanup.

This, of course, had John and Lane a little (upset). To give them credit, they did clean the trailer…making the beds and washing all the dishes. They did a great job. But they intentionally left one thing out.

I had at one time wandered into the house after fishing with a small cooler full of bait, which was mostly shrimp and a few small fish. There was probably about a pound of bait in that cooler. The top was on tight, but I had just left it in the trailer.

So, to get me back for leaving them with the cleanup John and Lane drove off and left the cooler in the house. It was summertime, and my dad did not come down to the trailer for over a month. Eventually he went down there with his friend who co-owned the place.

Upon entering my dad noticed the cooler just sitting in the middle of the den. He opened it…and according to his later testimony out came the worst smell in the history of mankind. It permeated the trailer instantly and just about had them sick.

My dad slammed the lid back on the cooler, but the smell was already set in at the trailer. Now, my dad would never normally waste anything, but he took that perfectly good cooler immediately to the dump and threw the whole thing, bait, cooler, and all into the pile.

When my dad got home all he knew was that I had left that cooler behind. I didn't even have time to blame it on John and Lane before he spoke. He came in and said just one single sentence, something he never has said to me any other time I can remember.

"I ought to kick your ass," said my dad.

And he probably should have. So John and Lane had the last laugh. But ever since then anytime I use the beach place my dad, in his sixties now, still interrogates me about making sure I have left nothing behind that might…smell. And I can't really blame him for that.

Uncle Tony, the Gun, and the Big Shark

I have an uncle named Tony who has always liked a good cold beer. When I was little (around 13) he would sometimes take me fishing with him on charter boats or piers and I would go buy his beer at the bar and carry it to him. They let me do that back then because everybody knew my uncle. Today a 13-year old trying to buy beer down at the beach would probably get thrown under the jail.

Anyway we had been out on a charter boat all day out of Calabash, NC which had (and still has) a great headboat fleet. We caught black sea bass on the bottom and I carried Uncle Tony plenty of beers.

We met some mates on the boat who were going to go shark fishing that night on the Cherry Grove Pier in northern SC just above Myrtle Beach. Back then sharking was more accepted on the beach piers than it is now and the Cherry Grove Pier had the best reputation for the big ones. In 1964 Walter Maxwell landed a 1,780-pound tiger shark from the end of that pier, an all-time shark record that stands to this day.

Well, Uncle Tony took me up on that pier to fish with the mates from the headboat that night. They tossed some mighty big baits into the water at the end of the pier (I don't know what they were using for bait but I remember it looked like half a cow). Then they proceed to talk some BS and drink more beer. I had fun fishing for little spot from the pier as the night got older.

Suddenly around midnight one of the rods started to scream. A big shark was on. The mates and Uncle Tony took turns fighting the big fish as it took so long they all got tired out. When we finally saw the beast down in the water (a huge hammerhead) a question came up. What do we do now?

It was decided we would beach the fish. So the mates walked it slowly all the way down the pier holding the rod up high and we all ended up on the shore. By this time everybody could see it, and we knew we were dealing with an enormous shark (in the end the fish weighed in right around 500 pounds, not far from a state record hammerhead in those days). A big crowd had gathered to watch. But the "experienced" mates were a bit scared (everyone had seen Jaws many times) and nobody knew how to calm and land the big shark, which was thrashing about in the surf and getting madder and madder.

Finally somebody said "Anybody got a gun?" It just so happened that there was a woman who had a little .22 pistol in her purse.

"Give me that gun," said Uncle Tony. Remember…this was after a loooooong day of beer drinking. The lady gave him the gun.

I will never forget the sight of my Uncle Tony wading into that surf, a .22 in one hand and a cold Coors Light beer in the other, going to kill the shark. As far as live entertainment, it was one of the highlights of my young life.

Soon we could see nothing in the dark, but everyone could hear the shark still thrashing around. Then there were three quick gunshots and bursts of light in the waves. After a few minutes, Uncle Tony emerged out of the surf.

"Drag that bastard up," he said, chugging the last of his Coors Light. And they did drag it up…a 500 pound hammerhead shark with three bullet holes in its head. I got to eat some really nice shark steaks, and I got an image I won't ever forget.

32. Saltwater Secrets: Catching Spanish on a Gold Hook Rig

As summer wanes Carolina saltwater anglers get in on some of the best Spanish mackerel action of the year. By using a 'gold-hook' rig you can gain an advantage over other fishermen and catch more Spanish.

Spanish mackerel are a much-prized saltwater gamefish that can be caught off the Carolinas' ocean fishing piers and nearshore boats. Spanish run in small schools during the late summer and early fall and hit shiny lures aggressively.

Many local Carolina anglers are familiar with throwing Gotcha pencil plugs for Spanish mackerel, usually using red headed and gold and silvered-bodied lures that Spanish favor. But there is a much better way of catching them from our ocean piers that will bring you a cooler full of Spanish, often when the pluggers are going home empty-handed.

You can use this rig off the deep end of our ocean piers among the Gotcha pluggers. South Carolina pier anglers have been throwing 'gold hook' rigs and catching

loads of Spanish for many years. Watching them, NC anglers have begun to make some imitations of their own.

Basically, to make a gold hook rig you begin the rig
by tying a bunch of number 4 gold hooks down a length of
leader (4# fluorocarbon is about right). You attach these
gold hooks using loops down the leader.

It is best to tie a loop at the top of the rig for attaching
the leader to the line running from your reel, although you
could use a swivel. I stay away from any hardware that
might spook the shy Spanish.

At the end of this rig you attach a diamond jig, a
Stingsilver spoon, or some other weighted lure with a treble
hook to your rig. You can even use a Gotcha plug at the end.
Some people tie the rig with a lead sinker on the end, but
that means you are missing out on the potential of a really
big Spanish hitting the trailing lure. I've caught some nice
Spanish on the jig or spoon at the end of this rig.

You cast this out as would a Gotcha plug, but you let
the rig hit the bottom. You then jig it back to you in swipes
of the rod tip. Spanish mackerel are attracted to the silver of
the plug but will as often hit one of the gold hooks. All of
that sparkle looks like a school of glass minnows which
Spanish feed heavily on.

With this rig you are virtually guaranteed to hook up
with any Spanish mackerel in the area of the pier. In fact,
multiple hook-ups may happen on a single cast, and it's
possible you could find yourself dealing with two or three
angry Spanish mackerel on the end of your line.

One warning, this lure also works on bluefish, which
is not a bad thing necessarily but blues may chomp or bite
off your mono rig forcing you to tie on another.

Sometimes the Spanish mackerel will hit Gotcha plugs and sometimes they won't. They can be right there but just feeding on smaller bait. If that is the case this version of the gold hook rig can be used to beat what the rest of the crowd is doing. On those occasions you will be the envy of all those anglers throwing plugs around you in vain.

33. Saltwater Secrets: Push Poling for Winter Redfish

Although some inshore saltwater anglers put away their fishing rods when cold weather arrives, others are still out there experiencing great action on schooled-up winter redfish. These redfish (also called red drum or puppy drum) provide year-round sport for shallow water anglers when other saltwater fishing targets have gone off to warmer waters.

Captain Mark Dickson of Shallow Minded Charters guides anglers to these winter redfish out of North Myrtle Beach, fishing in both North and South Carolina. Instead of stopping fishing when winter arrives Captain Dickson does some of his best business beginning in December, as redfish remain present inshore and feed on a host of different critters once the temperature rises during the day.

"During this time of year the redfish bunch into groups and follow the food," says Dickson. "On warmer days the mud minnows will come out of the shallows. Fiddler crabs still hang around on the darker banks and small grass shrimp stay here all year. There are still some finger mullet in the creeks. All of them are part of the winter diet of the redfish."

Winter redfish are schooled up very tightly in large pods, and guides like Dickson know they can be spooked easily. One of the biggest secrets to catching them is the approach you make before you ever wet a line. Redfish schools are sensitive to any noise or movement in the winter, so you have to be careful when you are targeting them.

"You have to use a stealthy approach," Dickson says. "It's important that you turn off your motor and use a long push pole to get to these fish. Otherwise they'll hear you coming and get spooked. Even running a trolling motor is no good."

Dickson turns off his motor and poles to the redfish once he's located a school. Then he goes to work. He once used live bait to catch redfish, even in the colder months, but with the improvements in modern day artificial lures he's gone over to using them more often.

"I used to fish mud minnows on jig heads," Dickson says, "but in the past few years we've gone with the Billy Bay Halo or the Gulp Shrimp lures. They are quicker and just as effective."

Anglers looking for redfish in the winter would do well to heed Dickson advice about the speed with which they retrieve these lures.

"You need to fish really, really slow in the winter for redfish," says Dickson. "Many of your fish will be caught when your lure isn't even moving. It's called dead sticking. Folks who do a bunch of jerking or add a lot of movement to the lure aren't going to catch much in the winter."

Huge redfish schools are often located in very shallow water during December and January in the Carolinas.

"Fishing for reds in the winter is sight fishing," says Dickson. "It's a lot like hunting. Even then sometimes you can see them but it will be so cold they won't bite. Other days you can catch all you want."

Contrary to many people's idea of fish going into deeper water for the winter, Dickson says the redfish school up in the shallows for safety.

"Redfish are lethargic in the winter which makes them easy prey for dolphins. Small red drum are a big part of the winter diet for the dolphins. Redfish will be in shallow water trying to stay away from them."

Dickson targets winter redfish with a 7-foot rod spooled with 20 lb Power Pro line, and he uses 20-lb fluorocarbon as a leader to his lures. Although red drum can get very large, most of the redfish Dickson encounters in the winter are under 27 inches. Both North and South Carolina have strict regulations regarding redfish, so Dickson does a lot of catch and release fishing for winter redfish. The hardy, powerful redfish provide great sport for his clients.

34. Tips for Taking a Kid Fishing

When the weather gets warm it's a great time to take a kid fishing. Here are some tips you can use when introducing children to this fun, interactive sport.

Pick a good fishing spot and an easy to catch species

You want don't want to introduce a child to fishing by surfcasting for trophy red drum or drowning big baits for chopper bluefish. Target species such as spot, croaker, sea mullet, and pinfish that will provide steady action. Choose quantity over quality to start a kid off—you needn't go after something to hang on the wall, just give them some chance to catch a few for themselves. It's better to leave them wanting more than bore them trying to bag a big one.

Keep children active and involved

Kids like hands on activities, and fishing is perfect for them. Give them small chores they can be responsible for, such as baiting their own hook or making sure everyone has a life jacket. Let them hold their own pole, but be sure to let them put it down if it starts to get heavy.

Avoid the temptation to do everything for them, as it's better to model what to do and only help them get started and again if they require aid. Don't be afraid to let them make a few mistakes. It takes a while to get some things, like casting, right and repetition is better than trying to for perfection the first time.

Go early in the day

Fishing with kids is a great morning activity, and school age children are used to early activities. They will be alert and enthusiastic. Putting a trip at the end of the day gives you the potential to end up with a tired, sleepy fishing partner.

Be aware of the elements

Kids need protection against things like sun and wind. You don't want a child's memory of their first fishing trip to be of a painful sunburn or a bad cold. Make sure you apply the sun block and that children are dressed appropriately for the weather. If it might be chilly don't be reluctant to bring a jacket or have a child dress in layers, as they can always shed clothes if they get hot.

Pack the essentials—food and drink

Kids won't have fun if they are thirsty or hungry. Bring along some tasty and nutritious snacks. Put plenty of water or juice in the cooler and avoid the soda which is less desirable for hydration.

Get in touch with nature

Fishing is an outdoor activity and you should take advantage of that fact. Don't confine your experience to casting out and reeling in. Show a child all the features of the habitat—the trails, the trees, the water. Make sure you also let them know the rules regarding safety and alertness.

Demonstrate environmental responsibility

Bring along a trash bag if trash cans won't be available. Make sure you explain size and creel limits for different fish species to a child and then make sure you observe them. Kids will get into catch and release fishing just as much as putting the fish in the cooler—if you explain to them the ideas behind conservation and being a responsible angler. At the same time, kids will get a kick out of keeping a few for the family to eat.

Make it a learning experience

Teach a child about wildlife and the sport, but don't give them information overload. Give them the basics and let them ask questions (which they will). If you are fishing in a very specific way, such as with lures or with a certain rig, let them know why. Fishing gives you a great excuse to teach a child all about the outdoors—just make sure to keep it fun.

Don't stay out too long

Children are not used to activities that take many hours to finish. Start out with short fishing trips and don't be reluctant to cut a trip a little short if concentration is waning. The hope is to leave them wanting to come back and looking forward to the next time.

35. Cyberfishing: Where to Get Current Fishing Reports and Tips

One of the great things about fishing today is the internet and the availability of a lot of solid and free information online. You can find up to date fishing reports, fishing articles, recipes, and the contact information for fishing piers and fishing guides all right there on your laptop computer, or even your mobile phone.

I can't list all of the many resources available on the internet for those wanting Carolina fishing information, but I can give you a real good start by telling you my favorite daily places to go for fishing information.

A Dash of Salty
http://saltyweeks.blogspot.com

This is my personal fishing blog. I have been running it for many years. It has links to hundreds of posts and articles about Carolina saltwater fishing (and also Carolina freshwater fishing) and I try to keep it updated with fishing reports as I get them in.

Surf and Salt
http://www.surfandsalt.com

This is the largest internet database of inshore surf and saltwater fishing articles and I run it! Here you will find much beyond the information in this book, including articles and recipes for some of the lesser known fish I didn't have room to put in this book. Surf and Salt also contains some articles about freshwater fishing for Carolina striped bass, largemouth bass, catfish, and more. Plus there are tons of additional seafood recipes.

Surf and Salt Tackle Shop
http://www.surfandsalt.com/tackle-shop.html

This is the online tackle shop that I run. It contains many of the baits, lures, and equipment I have recommended in this book. It is linked to Bass Pro Shops and if you purchase your gear here you will get it shipped directly to you at a very affordable price.

NC Waterman
http://www.ncwaterman.com

This is my favorite Carolina discussion and message board. I have been visiting it for many years and post on it often. Here you will find an amazing variety of reports, tips, tactics, information and also some lively (and sometimes downright testy) conversation about fisheries management and even politics. I love this site.

Outer Banks Fishing
http://www.outerbanksfishing.com

If you are going fishing on NC's famed Outer Banks check out this website first. There an updated fishing reports message board and lots of Outer Banks links for anglers.

Ocean Isle Fishing Center
http://www.oifc.com

This is an excellent website for anglers fishing the lower NC coast below the Wilmington area. Run by the family of Captain Brant McMullan the Ocean Isle Fishing Center is an all-in-one tackle shop, guide service, and fishing report center in beautiful Brunswick County.

Charleston Saltwater Fishing
http://www.charlestonsaltwaterfishing.com

If you are going fishing in the Charleston, SC area (and you should) you have to check out this great website, which has all the fishing report, guide recommendations, and Charleston inshore saltwater fishing information you need.

Pier and Surf
http://www.pierandsurf.com

Pier and Surf is another great discussion and message board site that covers many states beyond the Carolinas. It is a wonderful treasure trove for any inshore saltwater fisherman.

Ocean Crest Pier
http://www.oceancrestpiernc.com

This is the website for the Ocean Crest Pier, my favorite pier to fish in NC. It is on Oak Island in Brunswick

County. There are many great piers to fish on the Carolinas coast, but this is the one I frequent the most.

Bogue Inlet Pier
http://www.bogueinletpier.com

Bogue Inlet Pier at Emerald Isle, NC has one of the longest running pier websites. It includes some of the best up to date fishing reports you'll find on the internet. There are lots of great photos and current information about Emerald Isle Fishing.

Captain Smiley Fishing Charters
http://www.captainsmileyfishingcharters.com

Captain Patrick Kelly is a top-notch fishing guide out of North Myrtle Beach, SC whose picture is on the cover of this book! As you can tell by many of the pictures in this book Captain Smiley will put you on the fish in the lower NC and upper SC coastal areas. Captain Smiley has a great attitude and is in high demand as a lowcountry fishing guide.

Captain Mark Dickson
http://www.fishmyrtlebeach.com

Shallow Minded Guide Service is run by Captain Mark Dickson who also provided a lot of the pictures for this book. He is one of the best fishing guides on the Carolina coast, running out of the North Myrtle Beach area. Dickson updates his website and his Facebook page with plenty of current reports and pictures.

Custom Sound Charters
http://customsoundcharters.com

Captain Rick Caton is one of the most successful fishing guides on the Outer Banks of NC and he runs Custom Sound Charters. He updates his website with reports regularly. Caton is well-known for his unbelievable charters that deck huge striped bass, and he runs a lot of other types of charters and scenic trips as well.

Brunswick Beacon
http://www.brunswickbeacon.com

The *Brunswick Beacon* newspaper has featured my **Fishing Insider** column for many years. You can also check out Captain Brant McMullan's offshore report here and get a lot of information on southeastern NC beyond just fishing. The *Brunswick Beacon* is your source for local news, sports, events and information in Brunswick County, NC and surrounding areas.

Military Appreciation Day
http://www.militaryappreciationday.org

MAD is a great organization which started in Morehead City, NC and has spread out to amazing venues from there. These volunteers take US military service men and women on free fishing trips. Please check out their website and donate some money or time to this great cause if you can.

Fishermen In Support of Heroes
http://fishheroes.org

    This terrific non-profit organization hosts and sponsors fishing trips by volunteers for US military Wounded Warriors through donations of money, goods, and services. Please go to their website and help out this group which gives fishing adventures to our American heroes.

About the Author

Jeffrey Weeks is an award-winning North Carolina newspaper columnist who writes about saltwater and freshwater fishing, southern seafood cooking, and fisheries politics and management. He has been fishing the coasts of both Carolinas for over 35 years.

Jeffrey graduated from the University of North Carolina at Greensboro and taught high school civics, English, and journalism in North Carolina for 14 years. He lives in the Lake Norman area of NC but can often be found fishing out of the house in Ocean Isle Beach that his family has owned all of his life.

You can visit Jeffrey's website **Surf and Salt** at www.surfandsalt.com and find his blog **A Dash of Salty** at www.saltyweeks.blogspot.com. You can reach Jeffrey by email at saltyweeks@gmail.com.

Made in the USA
Lexington, KY
31 May 2014